Cake has been around for th[...]
very first cakes were made by [...]
stones. The cake went through a series of phases, first resembling a
cookie, then a pastry similar to cheesecake, and later, what we call fruit
bread. Finally, in the 17th century, the cake as we now know it —
with sponge-like layers and frosting — was born!

This baked treat has definitely stood the test of time, so it is no wonder
that cake is still our favorite way to celebrate any special occasion —
from birthdays to weddings to holidays. So, preheat your oven and tie
on your apron — it's time to bake cake!

Take the Cake

Bake, Take & Celebrate

from mixes • from scratch • Bundt cakes • tube cakes • coffee cakes • cupcakes • novelty cakes

Printed in the United States of America
by G&R Publishing Co.

Distributed By:

507 Industrial Street
Waverly, IA 50677

ISBN-13: 978-1-56383-281-9
ISBN-10: 1-56383-281-X
Item #7026

Table of Contents

Cake Basics

Preparation Tips

- Measure ingredients accurately for successful cake baking.

- It's easiest to separate eggs when they are cold.

- If beaten egg whites will be used to add volume to a cake, allow them to rest at room temperature for 20 to 30 minutes before beating.

Pan Tips

- Use the pan size recommended in the recipe for best results. If you must use a different pan, make an accurate conversion using the chart listed on page 6. For example, a 9 x 13″ pan can be substituted for two 8″ or 9″ round layers.

- For most cakes, if using a glass baking dish or dark coated metal pan instead of a shiny metal pan, lower the recommended oven temperature by 25° to prevent over-baking.

- When greasing and flouring cake pans for chocolate cakes, substitute cocoa powder for the flour to prevent a white coating on cake. If using a cake mix, substitute a bit of the dry cake mix for the flour.

- For best results, use ingredients at room temperature when possible.

- To remove a whole cake from the pan before decorating, cool it in the pan for just 10 to 15 minutes, then turn it out on a wire rack to cool completely. If cake remains in the pan longer than that, it tends to stick to the pan.

- A 10″ tube pan can be substituted for a Bundt pan; use the same baking times. However, do not substitute a Bundt pan for a tube pan when making cakes without shortening, such as traditional angel food cakes.

- Angel food and chiffon cakes are baked in ungreased pans. This allows the batter to cling to the pan's sides as it rises so it will not fall out of the pan when cooled upside down.

- Most cake will come out of the pan cleanly if you grease pan with a mixture of equal parts of shortening, vegetable oil and flour. Stir ingredients until smooth and store mixture in the refrigerator. Spread on the pan with a pastry brush before adding batter.

Baking Tips

- For best results, always preheat your oven to the correct temperature before baking cakes, unless directed otherwise.

- The center rack in the oven is the best place to bake cakes. If baking multiple pans on multiple racks, leave space between them and stagger rather than stack them, so heat can circulate evenly.

- Bake most cakes immediately after mixing them because cake batter does not store well.

- A cake containing butter or shortening is usually done when it shrinks back slightly from the sides of the pan, springs back when lightly pressed with fingertips, or when a toothpick inserted in the center of the cake comes out clean.

- Try not to disturb a cake for testing until it is almost done baking. If you pull the rack out of the oven before the cake is set, it may collapse.

- A dry cake is caused by over-baking. Test the cake at the shortest end of the recommended baking time. If it doesn't test done, return to the oven and re-check every few minutes.

- Foam cakes, like sponge, angel food and chiffon, must be cooled in the pan, upside down.

- Cool cakes and cupcakes completely before frosting them unless directed otherwise.

- Before turning a cake out on a cooling rack, spray the rack with nonstick vegetable oil to prevent sticking.

Cutting, Serving and Storage Tips

- Unfrosted cakes may be tightly wrapped and frozen for up to 6 weeks before eating. Unwrap, thaw at room temperature and frost.

- To prevent a freshly-baked cake from sticking to the serving plate, dust the empty plate with powdered sugar first.

- Let a frosted cake set up for 1 hour before cutting the cake.

- Use a wet knife to cut fresh cake more easily.

- Use a serrated knife to cut angel food or pound cakes.

- Refrigerate any leftover cake made with dairy products, such as sour cream, buttermilk and yogurt.

Common Baking Pans

Baking Pans and Equivalent Volumes

4-cup baking pan =
9″ pie plate
8″ round layer cake pan
7⅜ x 3⅝″ loaf pan

6-cup baking pan =
8″ or 9″ round layer cake pan
10″ pie plate
8½ x 3⅝″ loaf pan
7½″ fluted tube or Bundt pan

8-cup baking pan =
8″ square pan
7 x 11″ rectangular pan
9 x 5″ loaf pan

9-cup baking pan =
9″ fluted tube or Bundt pan

10-cup baking pan =
9″ square pan
7½ x 11¾″ rectangular pan
10 x 15″ jelly roll pan

12-cup baking pan =
9 x 13″ rectangular pan
9″ angel food cake pan
10″ fluted tube or Bundt pan
8″ springform pan

16-cup baking pan =
9″ springform pan

18-cup baking pan =
10″ angel food cake pan

Most Common Pan Sizes

rectangular pan – 9 x 13″
springform pan – 8″ or 9″
pie plate – 9″
round pan – 8″ or 9″
square pan – 8″ or 9″
jelly roll pan – 10 x 15″
angel food cake or tube pan – 10″
fluted tube or Bundt pan – 10″

loaf pan

springform pan

layer cake pan or pie plate

square pan

7 x 11″ rectangular pan

9 x 13″ rectangular pan

10 x 15″ jelly roll pan

*tube pan
(or angel food cake pan)*

*fluted tube pan
(or Bundt pan)*

Coffee Cakes

Tips for Baking Coffee Cakes

- Use shiny metal pans to bake coffee cakes with a golden tender crust. The pans reflect the heat to produce a delicate crust.

- Most coffee cakes should be cooled while they are still in the pan.

- Quantities of ingredients used for streusel toppings can be increased as desired for a thicker topping.

- When directed in a recipe to add dry and liquid ingredients alternately to a creamed mixture, end with the dry ingredients.

- Be sure butter is cold when cutting it into dry ingredients for a crumbly topping.

Rhubarb Almond Coffee Cake

Makes 1 (9 x 13˝) cake

Topping
½ C. sugar
2 T. butter, melted
½ C. chopped almonds

Cake
½ C. butter
1½ C. brown sugar
1 egg
½ tsp. almond extract
2 C. flour
1 tsp. baking soda
½ tsp. salt
1 C. sour cream
2 C. diced fresh rhubarb

Directions
Preheat oven to 350°. Grease a 9 x 13″ baking pan; set aside. In a small bowl, prepare the topping by combining sugar, melted butter and chopped almonds. Stir until crumbly; set aside. In a medium bowl, cream ½ cup butter, brown sugar, egg and almond extract. In another medium bowl, combine the flour, baking soda and salt; mix well. Add flour mixture to the creamed mixture alternately with the sour cream; mix well. Fold in diced rhubarb. Spread batter in prepared pan. Sprinkle prepared topping evenly over batter. Bake 45 to 50 minutes or until done. Cool coffee cake in pan; cut into squares to serve.

To serve as a dessert, stir a few drops of almond extract into whipped topping and place a dollop of topping on each piece.

Blueberry Brunch Coffee Cake

Makes 1 (10″) round cake

Sugar Topping
2 T. light brown sugar
⅛ tsp. ground nutmeg

Cake
¾ C. sugar
6 T. butter, softened
1 egg
1 egg white
1⅔ C. flour
¾ tsp. baking powder
½ tsp. baking soda
½ tsp. salt
½ C. low-fat buttermilk
¼ C. orange juice
1 tsp. grated lemon or orange peel
1 tsp. vanilla extract
1½ C. fresh blueberries

Creamy Topping
½ C. low-fat sour cream
1 tsp. vanilla extract
1 (6 to 8 oz.) carton low-fat
   vanilla yogurt
¾ C. fresh blueberries

Directions
Preheat oven to 350°. Coat bottom of a 10″ springform pan with nonstick cooking spray. Line bottom of pan with parchment or waxed paper. Coat paper and sides of pan with cooking spray, then dust with 1 tablespoon flour; set aside. In a small mixing bowl, combine brown sugar with nutmeg; set aside. In a medium mixing bowl, combine sugar with softened butter. Beat with an electric mixer for 5 minutes or until well blended. Add egg and egg white; beat well. In a medium bowl, combine flour, baking powder, baking soda and salt; set aside. In a small bowl, combine buttermilk, orange juice, lemon peel and 1 teaspoon vanilla extract. Alternately add flour mixture and buttermilk mixture to creamed mixture, beginning and ending with the flour mixture. Gently fold in 1½ cups blueberries. Spread batter in prepared pan. Sprinkle prepared topping mixture over batter. Bake 40 minutes or until toothpick inserted in center of cake comes out clean. Cool cake in pan 10 minutes on wire rack; remove sides of pan.

In a small bowl, combine sour cream, 1 teaspoon vanilla and yogurt. Serve cake warm or cool with creamy topping and ¾ cup fresh blueberries. Refrigerate any leftover cake.

9

Honey Bun Coffee Cake

Makes 1 (9 x 13″) cake

Cake
1 (18.2 oz.) pkg. yellow cake mix
⅔ C. vegetable oil
4 eggs
1 (8 oz.) carton sour cream
   or plain yogurt

Filling
1 C. brown sugar
⅓ C. chopped pecans
2 tsp. ground cinnamon

Icing
1 C. powdered sugar, sifted
1 T. plus 1 tsp. milk
1 tsp. vanilla extract

Directions
Preheat oven to 350°. Grease and lightly flour a 9 x 13″ baking pan; set aside. In a large mixing bowl, combine dry cake mix, oil, eggs and sour cream. Beat with an electric mixer at low speed for 30 seconds, then at medium speed for 2 additional minutes, scraping bowl occasionally. Spread half the batter in prepared pan. In a small bowl, combine brown sugar, pecans and cinnamon. Sprinkle brown sugar mixture over batter in pan. Drizzle remaining batter evenly over brown sugar mixture, then carefully spread to fill uncovered spaces. Bake 44 to 48 minutes or until deep golden brown.

In a small bowl, combine powdered sugar, milk and vanilla extract until thin enough to spread. While cake is still warm, prick surface of cake repeatedly with a fork. Spread powdered sugar icing over cake. Cool cake completely. Refrigerate any leftover cake.

Spicy Buttermilk Coffee Cake

Makes 1 (9 x 13″) cake

Topping
1 tsp. ground cinnamon
½ C. chopped pecans

Cake
2⅓ C. flour
¾ C. sugar
1 C. brown sugar
1 tsp. ground nutmeg
1 tsp. salt
¾ C. vegetable oil
1 C. buttermilk
1 tsp. baking soda
1 egg, beaten
1 tsp. maple or burnt sugar
   flavoring

Directions
Preheat oven to 350°. Grease and flour a 9 x 13″ baking pan; set aside. In a small bowl, combine cinnamon and chopped pecans; set aside. In a medium bowl, combine flour, sugar, brown sugar, nutmeg, salt and oil; stir well. Remove ¾ cup of this mixture and add it to the nut mixture to use as a topping; set mixture aside. To remaining sugar mixture, add buttermilk, baking soda, egg and flavoring; mix well. Pour batter into prepared pan. Sprinkle topping mixture evenly over batter. Bake 35 to 40 minutes. Let cool for at least 15 minutes before cutting into squares. Serve warm or cold. Refrigerate any leftover cake.

Overnight Company Coffee Cake

Makes 1 (9 x 13″) cake

Topping

½ C. brown sugar
½ tsp. ground cinnamon
½ C. chopped walnuts

Cake

⅔ C. butter, softened
1 C. sugar
½ C. brown sugar
2 eggs
2 C. flour
1 tsp. baking powder
½ tsp. baking soda
1 tsp. ground cinnamon
1 C. buttermilk

Directions

Prepare this batter the night before. Lightly grease a 9 x 13″ baking pan; set aside. In a small bowl, mix ½ cup brown sugar, ½ teaspoon cinnamon and walnuts; set topping aside. In a large bowl, cream together butter, sugar and ½ cup brown sugar. Beat in eggs until well blended. In a separate bowl, combine flour, baking powder, baking soda and 1 teaspoon cinnamon. Alternately add flour mixture and buttermilk to creamed mixture, stirring well. Spread batter in prepared pan. Sprinkle topping over batter. Cover and refrigerate overnight.

To bake the next morning, preheat oven to 350°. If desired, sprinkle a little more brown sugar on top of batter in pan. Bake 40 to 50 minutes or until a toothpick inserted in center of cake comes out clean. Refrigerate any leftover cake.

Citrus Coffee Cake

Makes 1 (10˝) Bundt cake

Cake

3 C. flour
1½ C. sugar
¾ C. brown sugar
3 T. grated orange peel
4 tsp. grated lemon peel
3 to 4 tsp. chopped fresh rosemary
1½ tsp. baking soda
½ tsp. salt
2 eggs
1 C. buttermilk
¾ C. butter, melted
¼ C. pine nuts

Glaze

1 C. powdered sugar, sifted
4 tsp. orange juice
Pine nuts, optional

Directions

Preheat oven to 350°. Coat a 10˝ Bundt pan with nonstick cooking spray; set aside. In a large bowl, combine flour, sugar, brown sugar, orange peel, lemon peel, rosemary, baking soda and salt; set aside. In a medium bowl, combine eggs, buttermilk and melted butter; stir well. Add buttermilk mixture to flour mixture and stir just until combined. Fold in pine nuts. Spoon batter into prepared pan. Bake 45 to 50 minutes or until a toothpick inserted in center of cake comes out clean. Cool cake in pan for 15 minutes, then invert cake onto a serving platter.

To make glaze, in a small bowl, combine powdered sugar and enough orange juice to make a drizzling consistency. Drizzle glaze over warm cake and, if desired, sprinkle with additional pine nuts. Serve cake warm. Refrigerate any leftover cake.

Sweet Lemon Cake with Berries

Makes 1 (9 x 5″) loaf cake

Cake

1½ C. flour
¼ tsp. baking powder
⅛ tsp. baking soda
½ C. butter, softened
1 C. sugar
3 eggs
½ C. sour cream
1 tsp. grated lemon peel

Glaze, optional

⅓ C. lemon juice
⅓ C. sugar
Fresh berries
Powdered sugar, optional

Directions

Preheat oven to 325°. Grease and lightly flour a 9 x 5″ loaf pan; set aside. In a small bowl, combine flour, baking powder and baking soda; set aside. In a large mixing bowl, combine butter and 1 cup sugar. Beat with an electric mixer at high speed about 5 minutes or until light and fluffy. Reduce speed to low and beat in eggs, one at a time, until well blended. Alternately add flour mixture and sour cream to butter mixture. Stir in lemon peel by hand. Pour batter into prepared pan. Bake 1 to 1¼ hours or until a toothpick inserted in center of cake comes out clean.

If desired, prepare glaze in a cup by mixing lemon juice and ⅓ cup sugar. Drizzle lemon glaze evenly over warm cake in pan. Let cake cool in pan on wire rack. If desired, sprinkle powdered sugar on top. Serve slices of cake with fresh berries on top.

Chocolate Spice Coffee Cake

Makes 1 (9 x 13″) cake

Cake and Topping

3 C. flour
2 C. sugar
1 C. butter or margarine, cold
4 tsp. unsweetened cocoa powder
1 T. ground cinnamon
½ tsp. ground nutmeg
⅛ tsp. ground cloves
1 tsp. baking soda
½ tsp. baking powder
⅛ tsp. salt
1 C. raisins
½ C. chopped nuts
2 C. buttermilk

Directions

Preheat oven to 350°. Grease a 9 x 13″ baking pan; set aside. In a large bowl, combine flour and sugar. Using a pastry blender or two knives, cut in butter until crumbly. Set aside 1¼ cups of the mixture for topping. To the remaining mixture, add cocoa powder, cinnamon, nutmeg, cloves, baking soda, baking powder and salt; mix well. Stir in raisins and nuts. Make a well in the center and pour in buttermilk. Stir just until moistened. Spread batter in prepared pan. Sprinkle with reserved crumb mixture. Bake 35 to 40 minutes or until a toothpick inserted in center of cake comes out clean. Cool cake before cutting and serving.

Banana Coffee Cake with Crunchy Topping

Makes 1 (9″) round cake

Cake

1⅓ C. flour

½ tsp. salt

½ tsp. baking powder

¼ tsp. baking soda

1 C. mashed ripe banana (about 2 large bananas)

¾ C. sugar

3 T. vegetable oil

1 tsp. vanilla extract

¼ tsp. ground nutmeg

1 egg

Topping

¼ C. dark brown sugar

2 tsp. butter

2 T. chopped macadamia nuts, toasted*

2 T. flaked coconut

Directions

Preheat oven to 350°. Coat a 9″ round baking pan with nonstick cooking spray. Line the bottom of pan with waxed paper and spray paper with cooking spray; set aside. In a medium bowl, combine flour, salt, baking powder and baking soda; stir well to mix. In a medium mixing bowl, combine mashed banana, sugar, oil, vanilla extract, nutmeg and egg. Beat with an electric mixer at medium speed for 1 minute. Add flour mixture to banana mixture and beat until blended. Pour batter into prepared pan. Bake 30 minutes or until a toothpick inserted in center of cake comes out clean. Cool cake in pan for 10 minutes; then remove cake from pan and carefully peel off waxed paper.

In a small saucepan over medium heat, combine brown sugar, 1 tablespoon water and butter. Bring to a boil and cook for 1 minute, stirring constantly. Remove from heat and stir in nuts and coconut. Spread over cake and serve cake warm.

To toast, place chopped macadamia nuts in a single layer on a baking sheet. Bake at 350° for approximately 10 minutes or until golden brown.

Filled Sour Cream Coffee Cake

Makes 1 (10″) Bundt cake

Cake

½ C. butter
1 C. sugar
½ C. brown sugar
1 C. sour cream
2 eggs
1 tsp. vanilla extract
2 C. flour
1 tsp. baking powder
1 tsp. baking soda

Filling

1 tsp. ground cinnamon
¼ C. brown sugar

Glaze

1 C. powdered sugar, sifted
2 to 4 T. milk

Directions

Preheat oven to 350°. Grease and flour a 10″ Bundt pan; set aside. In a large mixing bowl, beat together butter, sugar, ½ cup brown sugar, sour cream, eggs and vanilla extract with an electric mixer at medium speed. In a separate bowl, combine flour, baking powder and baking soda; mix well. Add flour mixture to creamed mixture and blend until smooth. To make filling, in a small bowl, combine cinnamon and ¼ cup brown sugar; set aside. Pour half of the cake batter into prepared pan. Sprinkle brown sugar mixture on top of batter in pan. Cover with remaining batter. Bake 45 to 50 minutes. Cool cake in pan.

In a small bowl, make a thick glaze by mixing powdered sugar with 2 tablespoons milk until smooth. Add more milk as needed until glaze reaches desired consistency. Pour glaze over cooled cake.

Applesauce Raisin Cake

Cake

½ C. shortening

1½ C. sugar

2 eggs, beaten

½ tsp. salt

1 tsp. ground cinnamon

½ tsp. ground cloves

2½ C. flour

1½ C. applesauce

1 tsp. baking soda

1 C. raisins

½ C. chopped nuts, optional

Directions

Preheat oven to 350°. Generously grease a 9 x 5″ loaf pan; set aside. In a large mixing bowl, cream together shortening and sugar with an electric mixer at medium speed. Reduce speed and add eggs, salt, cinnamon and cloves; mix well. Alternately add flour and applesauce to creamed mixture until well blended. Dissolve baking soda in 2 tablespoons hot water. Pour soda mixture into batter and mix well. Fold in raisins and nuts. Pour batter into prepared pan and bake about 1 hour. Cool cake completely and cut into slices.

Almond and Raspberry Coffee Cake

Makes 1 (9˝) square cake

Streusel

⅓ C. flour

¼ C. sugar

¼ C. butter or margarine, cold

⅓ c. slivered almonds

Cake

¼ C. butter or margarine, softened

¾ C. sugar

1 C. milk

2 C. flour

2 tsp. baking powder

1 tsp. vanilla extract

½ tsp. salt

1 egg

3 to 4 oz. almond paste, finely chopped, divided

1 C. fresh raspberries, divided

Directions

Preheat oven to 350°. Grease a 9˝ square baking pan; set aside. In a small bowl, mix the streusel by combining flour and sugar. With a pastry blender or two knives, cut in butter until crumbly. Stir in almonds; set streusel aside.

In a large mixing bowl, cream together butter and sugar with an electric mixer at low speed. Add milk, flour, baking powder, vanilla extract, salt and egg; mix at low speed for 30 seconds. Beat at medium speed for 2 minutes, scraping bowl frequently. Spread half of cake batter in prepared pan. Sprinkle with half the chopped almond paste and ½ cup raspberries. Spread remaining batter on top. Sprinkle remaining almond paste and raspberries on top of batter. Sprinkle with streusel mixture. Bake 50 minutes or until a toothpick inserted in center of cake comes out clean. Serve cake warm or cool.

Easy Strawberry Coffee Cake

Makes 1 (8″) square cake

Topping
½ C. flour
½ C. sugar
¼ C. butter, cold
¼ C. chopped pecans

Cake
1 C. flour
½ C. sugar
2 tsp. baking powder
½ tsp. salt
1 egg
½ C. milk
2 T. butter, melted
1½ C. sliced fresh strawberries

Directions
Preheat oven to 375°. Grease an 8″ baking pan; set aside. In a medium bowl, prepare topping by mixing together flour and sugar. With a pastry blender or two knives, cut in butter until crumbly. Stir in pecans. Set topping aside.

In a large bowl, prepare cake batter by combining flour, sugar, baking powder and salt; mix well. In a small bowl, beat together the egg, milk and melted butter. Stir milk mixture into flour mixture just until moistened and well blended. Pour batter into prepared pan. Top with strawberries. Sprinkle topping mixture over strawberries. Bake 30 to 35 minutes or until a toothpick inserted in center of cake comes out clean. Cool in pan for 5 to 10 minutes before cutting into squares. Serve warm.

Cakes from Mixes

Tips for Baking Cakes from Mixes

• Note the size of a packaged mix before proceeding with recipes. Some package mixes are for snack-sized cakes; others are for two-layer or 9 x 13″ cakes.

• A prepared packaged cake mix yields about 4½ cups of batter. To make two equal layers, use about 2¼ cups of batter in each layer.

• Some cake mixes have pudding added for extra moisture. Unless otherwise noted, use plain cake mixes for best results.

• To cut a cake into two layers, chill it first. Then mark the middle with toothpicks for a cutting guide and cut with a long serrated knife.

Fudge-Topped Crème de Menthe Cake

Makes 1 (9 x 13˝) cake

Cake

1 (18.2 oz.) pkg. white cake mix

Vegetable oil, eggs and water as directed on cake mix package

3 T. crème de menthe

Topping

1 (11.7 oz.) jar fudge ice cream topping, slightly warmed

2 to 3 T. crème de menthe

1 (12 oz.) carton whipped topping

Directions

Preheat oven to 350°. Grease and flour a 9 x 13˝ baking pan; set aside. In a large mixing bowl, combine cake mix with oil, eggs and water as directed on the cake mix package. Mix at low speed, adding 3 tablespoons crème de menthe. Mix at high speed for the time listed on package. Bake cake as directed. Cool cake in pan completely.

Spread fudge topping over cooled cake. Add 2 to 3 tablespoons of crème de menthe to whipped topping and stir until well blended. Spread whipped topping over fudge layer. Refrigerate before serving. Refrgerate any leftover cake.

Low-Fat Chocolate Cake

Makes 1 (10˝) Bundt cake

Cake

1 (18.2 oz.) pkg. reduced-fat devil's food cake mix

1 C. nonfat plain yogurt

½ C. orange juice

2 eggs

2 T. unsweetened applesauce

2 T. grated orange peel

1 tsp. ground cinnamon

Chocolate Glaze

(recipe on page 124) or frostng of your choice

Directions

Preheat oven to 350°. Coat a 10˝ Bundt pan with nonstick cooking spray or shortening, then dust with flour; set aside. In a large mixing bowl, combine the cake mix, yogurt, orange juice, eggs, applesauce, orange peel, cinnamon and ½ cup water. Beat at low speed for 1 minute, scraping bowl constantly. Pour batter into prepared pan. Bake 50 to 55 minutes or until a toothpick inserted in center of cake comes out clean. Cool cake for 10 minutes before inverting onto a wire rack to cool completely.

Prepare Chocolate Glaze (recipe on page 124) and drizzle over cake, or frost as desired or sprinkle top with powdered sugar.

German Chocolate Flip Cake

Cake

1 C. flaked coconut

1 C. chopped pecans

1 (18.2 oz.) pkg. German chocolate cake mix

Vegetable oil, eggs and water as directed on cake mix package

1 (8 oz.) pkg. cream cheese

½ C. butter

3¾ C. powdered sugar, sifted

Powdered sugar, sifted, optional

Directions

Preheat oven to 350°. Spray a 9 x 13˝ baking pan with nonstick cooking spray. Line pan bottom with waxed paper; spray waxed paper. Sprinkle coconut and pecans evenly over bottom of prepared pan; set aside. In a large mixing bowl, combine cake mix with oil, eggs and water as directed on the cake mix package. Pour cake batter evenly over coconut and nut mixture. In a large saucepan over low heat, combine cream cheese and butter, stirring until cheese and butter are melted. Stir in powdered sugar until well blended and smooth. Pour mixture evenly over cake batter. Bake 40 to 45 minutes or until a toothpick inserted in center of cake comes out clean. Cool in pan for 10 minutes. Invert cake on a platter and remove waxed paper. Cool cake completely. Sprinkle additional sifted powdered sugar over cake before serving.

Double Chocolate Mint Cake

Makes 2 (9˝) round layers

Cake

1 (18.2 oz.) pkg. chocolate
  cake mix

Vegetable oil, eggs and water as
  directed on cake mix package

20 chocolate-covered mint patties

Topping

2 (16 oz.) containers prepared
  creamy chocolate frosting

10 chocolate-covered mint patties

Directions

Preheat oven to 350°. Grease and
flour two 9˝ round baking pans;
set aside. In a large mixing bowl,
combine cake mix, oil, eggs and
water as directed on the cake
mix package. Divide batter evenly
into prepared pans. Unwrap 20
mint patties and place 10 patties
in a circle over batter of each cake
before baking. Bake about 30
minutes or until cake springs back
to a light touch. Cool cakes for
10 minutes, then carefully remove
from pans. Cool cakes completely.

Spread chocolate frosting on one
side of each of the cake layers.
Arrange 10 more unwrapped
candies on top of the frosting on
one of the layers. Invert the other
layer and set it on top of the first
layer, frosting side down. Spread
remaining frosting over top and
sides of cake.

Chocolate Caramel Better than Anything Cake

Makes 1 (9 x 13″) cake

Cake

1 (18.2 oz.) pkg. chocolate cake mix
Vegetable oil, eggs and water as directed on cake mix package

Toppings

1 (14 oz.) can sweetened condensed milk
1 (12 oz.) jar caramel or caramel fudge ice cream topping
1 (8 oz.) carton whipped topping
¾ C. chocolate-covered toffee bits

Directions

Preheat oven to 350°. Grease and flour a 9 x 13″ baking pan; set aside. In a large mixing bowl, combine cake mix, oil, eggs and water as directed on cake mix package. Pour cake batter into prepared pan and bake as directed. Cool cake completely.

Use the handle of a wooden spoon to poke holes into the top of cake about every inch. Slowly pour can of sweetened condensed milk into holes in cake. Pour jar of caramel topping over cake. Spread whipped topping over cake. Sprinkle toffee pieces over whipped topping. Refrigerate until serving. Refrigerate any leftover cake.

Tasty Tropical Cake

Makes 1 (9 x 13″) cake

Cake

1 (18.2 oz.) pkg. yellow cake mix

Vegetable oil, eggs and water as
   directed on cake mix package

Toppings

1 (14 oz.) can cream of coconut

1 (14 oz.) can sweetened
   condensed milk

1 (20 oz.) can crushed pineapple

1 (8 oz.) carton whipped topping

1 C. flaked coconut

Directions

Preheat oven to 350°. Grease and
flour a 9 x 13″ baking pan; set aside.
In a large mixing bowl, combine
cake mix with oil, eggs and water
as directed on the cake mix package.
Bake cake as directed.

Remove cake from oven and use
the handle of a wooden spoon to
poke holes into the top of cake
about every inch. Slowly pour
cream of coconut, then sweetened
condensed milk into the holes and
all over the cake. Pour crushed
pineapple with juice over cake.
Refrigerate until chilled.

In a medium bowl, mix whipped
topping and flaked coconut
together. Spread mixture over cake,
cover and refrigerate until serving.
Serve cold. This cake is best if made
the day before serving.

Pineapple and Orange Layer Cake

Makes 2 (9˝) round layers

Cake

1 (18.2 oz.) pkg. yellow cake mix

Vegetable oil, eggs and water as directed on cake mix package

1 (11 oz.) can mandarin oranges, drained

Filling and Topping

1 (20 oz.) can unsweetened crushed pineapple, drained

1 (3.4 oz.) pkg. vanilla instant pudding mix

1 (12 oz.) carton whipped topping

Directions

Preheat oven to 350°. Grease and flour two 9˝ round baking pans; set aside. In a large mixing bowl, combine cake mix with oil, eggs and water as directed on the cake mix package. Add mandarin oranges and stir until well mixed. Pour batter into prepared pans. Bake 25 to 30 minutes or until a toothpick inserted in center of cake comes out clean. Cool for 10 minutes before removing cakes from pans to wire racks to cool completely.

In a medium bowl, stir together pineapple and pudding mix. Fold in whipped topping. Spread part of pineapple mixture between the layers of cake and spread remaining mixture over top and sides of cake. Store cake in refrigerator.

Creamy Coconut Three-Milk Cake ("Tres Leches")

Makes 1 (9 x 13″) cake

Cake

1 (18.2 oz.) pkg. white or yellow cake mix

1 T. vegetable oil

2 tsp. vanilla extract, divided

4 eggs

Topping

1 (14 oz.) can sweetened condensed milk

½ C. canned cream of coconut (not coconut milk)

1 C. whipping cream

1 T. vanilla extract

1 (16 oz.) container whipped topping

Flaked coconut, toasted*, optional

Strawberry slices, optional

Kiwi, peeled and chopped, optional

Directions

Preheat oven to 350°. Spray a 9 x 13″ baking pan with nonstick cooking spray; set aside. In a large mixing bowl, combine cake mix, 1¼ cups water, oil, 2 teaspoons vanilla extract and eggs; beat at low speed for 30 seconds. Beat at medium speed for 2 minutes, scraping bowl occasionally. Pour batter into prepared pan. Bake 29 to 35 minutes or until edges are golden brown and a toothpick inserted in center of cake comes out clean. Cool cake in pan for 1 hour.

With a long-tined fork, poke holes into top of cooled cake every ½″. In a medium bowl, mix sweetened condensed milk, cream of coconut, whipping cream and remaining 1 tablespoon of vanilla extract until well blended. Pour mixture evenly over top of cake and into holes, using all of mixture. Cover and refrigerate 4 hours or overnight so cake can soak up liquid.

Spread whipped topping over cake and sprinkle toasted coconut on top, if desired. Serve cold with fresh fruit.

To toast, spread coconut in a shallow baking pan. Bake 7 to 10 minutes, stirring frequently, until lightly brown.

Strawberry Bundt Cake

Cake

1 (18.2 oz.) pkg. strawberry
   cake mix
1 (3 oz.) pkg. coconut cream
   instant pudding mix
½ C. vegetable oil
¼ tsp. strawberry flavoring
¼ tsp. coconut flavoring
4 eggs

Almond Glaze

(recipe on page 123)

Directions

Preheat oven to 350°. Grease and flour a 10″ Bundt pan; set aside. In a large mixing bowl, combine cake mix and pudding mix. Add 1 cup water, oil, strawberry flavoring and coconut flavoring; beat at low speed until combined. Add eggs, one at a time, beating well at high speed after each addition. The batter will be thin. Pour batter into prepared pan. Bake 45 to 50 minutes. Cool cake for 20 minutes before removing carefully from pan.

Prepare Almond Glaze (recipe on page 123), but substitute vanilla or coconut flavoring for the almond extract, if desired. Drizzle glaze over partially cooled cake. Cool cake completely before slicing

Strawberry Delight

Makes 1 (9 x 13˝) cake

Cake

1 (18.2 oz.) pkg. white cake mix
2 T. flour
1 (3 oz.) pkg. strawberry gelatin powder
¾ C. vegetable oil
1 (10 oz.) pkg. frozen sliced strawberries in syrup, thawed
4 eggs

Topping

½ (10 oz.) pkg. frozen sliced strawberries in syrup, thawed
¼ C. butter, melted
3¾ C. powdered sugar

Directions

Preheat oven to 350°. Grease a 9 x 13″ baking pan; set aside. In a large mixing bowl, combine cake mix, flour, strawberry gelatin powder, oil, 1 package strawberries with syrup and ¼ cup water. Mix together at low speed. Add eggs, one at a time, and beat at medium speed for about 2 minutes or until batter is smooth and silky. Do not overbeat. Pour mixture into prepared pan and bake 30 to 35 minutes or until cake does not jiggle when moved. Cool cake in the pan for 15 to 20 minutes.

Place half of a package of thawed strawberries with syrup into a medium mixing bowl and add melted butter; stir together. Add powdered sugar gradually, beating well with an electric mixer after each addition until somewhat thick. Pour mixture over partially cooled cake and serve immediately. Leftover cake can be warmed slightly in the microwave.

Rum Bundt Cake

Makes 1 (10˝) Bundt cake

Cake

1 C. chopped pecans

1 (18.2 oz.) pkg. yellow cake mix

1 (3.4 oz.) pkg. vanilla instant pudding mix

4 eggs, room temperature

½ C. vegetable oil

½ C. dark or golden rum (not spiced)

Glaze

¼ C. butter

½ C. sugar

¼ C. dark or golden rum (not spiced)

Directions

Preheat oven to 375°. Grease and flour a 10˝ Bundt or tube pan. Sprinkle chopped nuts over bottom of pan. In a large bowl, mix together cake mix, pudding mix, eggs, ½ cup water, oil and ½ cup rum until well blended. Pour batter over nuts in prepared pan. Bake 60 minutes. Remove from oven and cool in pan for 20 minutes. Carefully run a long sharp knife around the edge of the cake and invert cake onto a serving plate. With a wooden skewer or long-tined fork, poke holes all over the top of cake and set aside.

In a small saucepan over medium heat, melt butter. Stir in 2 tablespoons water and sugar. Bring mixture to a boil and cook for 5 minutes, stirring constantly. Remove from heat and stir in ¼ cup rum. While cake is still warm, spoon and brush glaze evenly over top, allowing it to seep into holes, down cake sides and into center. Repeat to use all glaze. Let cake absorb glaze and cool completely before cutting.

Quick Butterscotch Cake

Makes 1 (10″) Bundt cake

Cake

1 (18.2) oz. pkg. white cake mix

1 (3.4 oz.) pkg. butterscotch instant pudding mix

1 C. milk

½ C. vegetable oil

4 egg whites

¼ C. powdered sugar

Directions

Preheat oven to 350°. Grease and flour a 10″ Bundt pan; set aside. In a large mixing bowl, combine cake mix, pudding mix, milk, oil and egg whites. With an electric mixer, beat at low speed for 30 seconds, then at medium speed for 2 additional minutes. Pour batter into prepared pan. Bake 50 to 60 minutes or until a toothpick inserted in center of cake comes out clean. Cool cake in the pan for 10 minutes, then carefully invert cake onto a wire rack and cool completely. Sprinkle powdered sugar over top before serving.

Chocolate-Frosted Cherry Cake

Makes 1 (9 x 13˝) cake

Cake

1 (10 to 12 oz.) jar maraschino cherries with juice

1 (18.2 oz.) pkg. white cake mix

Vegetable oil, eggs and water as directed on cake mix package

Frosting

Cream Cheese Frosting (recipe on page 122)

1 C. milk chocolate chips

Directions

Preheat oven to 350°. Grease and flour a 9 x 13″ baking pan; set aside. In a measuring cup, reserve cherry juice. Add water as needed to obtain total amount of water listed on cake mix directions. In a large mixing bowl, combine cake mix, oil, eggs and cherry juice/water combination as directed on cake mix package. Cut cherries into fourths; fold cherry pieces into cake batter. Spread batter in prepared pan and bake as directed on package. Cool cake completely in pan.

Prepare Cream Cheese Frosting (recipe on page 122) and set aside. In a small microwave-safe bowl, place chocolate chips and microwave for 30 seconds. Stir and repeat until chocolate is melted. Add melted chocolate to prepared Cream Cheese Frosting and stir well. Spread frosting immediately on cooled cake. Refrigerate any leftover cake.

Raspberries and Cream Layer Cake

Makes 3 (8″) round layers

Cake

1 (18.2 oz.) pkg. lemon or yellow
  cake mix
2 eggs
1 egg white
¼ C. unsweetened applesauce

Fillings and Toppings

Whipped Cream Frosting
  (recipe on page 111)
¾ to 1 C. raspberry spreadable fruit
Chocolate syrup, optional
Fresh raspberries, optional

Directions

Preheat oven to 350°. Coat three
8″ round baking pans with nonstick
cooking spray; set aside. In a large
mixing bowl, use an electric mixer
to combine cake mix, eggs, egg
white, applesauce and 1¼ cups
water. Beat at low speed for 30
seconds or until mixed. Beat at
medium speed for 2 minutes,
scraping bowl occasionally. Pour
an equal amount of batter into
prepared pans. Bake 25 to 35
minutes or until a toothpick
inserted in center of cake comes out
clean. Cool for 10 minutes before
removing cakes from pans to wire
racks to cool completely.

Prepare Whipped Cream Frosting
(recipe on page 111). Place one cake
layer on a serving plate. Spread top
of cake with half of the spreadable
fruit. Spread a third of the frosting
on top of fruit. Place second cake
layer on top. Spread top of cake
with remaining spreadable fruit
and another third of frosting. Place
remaining cake layer on top and
spread with remaining frosting.
Drizzle chocolate syrup over frosting
and garnish with fresh raspberries,
if desired.

Quick Rhubarb Upside-Down Cake

Makes 1 (9 x 13˝) cake

Cake and Topping

1 (18.2 oz.) pkg. yellow cake mix

Vegetable oil, eggs and water as directed on cake mix package

3 C. chopped rhubarb, ½˝ to 1˝ pieces

1 C. sugar

1 C. whipping cream

Directions

Preheat oven to 350°. Grease and flour a 9 x 13˝ baking pan; set aside. In a large mixing bowl, combine cake mix, oil, eggs and water as directed on the cake mix package. Pour batter into prepared pan. In a medium bowl, combine chopped rhubarb and sugar. Spoon sugared rhubarb evenly over batter. Drizzle whipping cream over rhubarb and batter. Bake 40 to 50 minutes or until a toothpick inserted in center of cake comes out clean. Cool cake completely before turning it out onto a serving platter. Refrigerate any leftover cake.

Apricot Lemon Cake

Cake

1 (18.2 oz.) pkg. lemon cake mix
1 C. apricot nectar
¾ C. vegetable oil
⅓ C. sugar
4 eggs

Lemon Glaze
(recipe on page 124)

Directions

Preheat oven to 325°. Grease a 10″ Bundt or tube pan well. In a large mixing bowl, combine cake mix, apricot nectar, oil and sugar; mix well. Add eggs, one at a time, beating well after each addition. Pour batter into prepared pan. Bake about 60 minutes. Let cake cool in pan for 10 minutes, then invert cake onto a serving plate.

Prepare Lemon Glaze (recipe on page 124) and pour over cake while still warm.

Variation
This cake can also be made using an orange cake mix and *Orange Glaze* (recipe variation on page 124).

Sour Cream Raspberry Bundt Cake

Makes 1 (10˝) Bundt cake

Cake

1 (10 oz.) pkg. sweetened raspberries, thawed

1 (18.2 oz.) pkg. golden butter recipe cake mix

⅓ C. sugar

1 C. sour cream

½ C. vegetable oil

4 eggs

Glaze

2 to 2½ C. powdered sugar

¼ C. reserved raspberry syrup

¼ tsp. lemon flavoring

Directions

Do not preheat oven. Grease and flour a 10″ Bundt pan; set aside. Drain raspberries well, reserving ¼ cup of syrup in a small bowl; set berries and reserved syrup aside. In a large mixing bowl, combine cake mix, sugar, sour cream, oil and eggs. Beat with electric mixer at low speed until blended. Beat at medium speed for 4 additional minutes. Pour ⅔ of the batter into prepared pan. Drop raspberries on top of batter. Top with remaining cake batter. Place in cold oven and set temperature to 325°. Bake for 50 to 55 minutes or until a toothpick inserted in center of cake comes out clean. Cool cake in pan for 10 minutes then invert cake onto a wire rack to cool completely.

Place 2 cups powdered sugar in a small bowl and slowly add reserved raspberry syrup while stirring. Add lemon flavoring and mix well. Add more powdered sugar as needed until glaze reaches desired consistency. Spoon glaze over top of cooled cake.

Dreamy Orange Cake

Makes 1 (9 x 13″) cake

Cake

1 (18.2 oz.) pkg. vanilla cake mix
1 (12 oz.) can orange soda
2 eggs
1 (3 oz.) pkg. orange gelatin
  powder

Creamy Orange Frosting
(recipe on page 120)

Directions

Preheat oven to 350°. Coat a
9 x 13″ baking pan with nonstick
cooking spray; set aside. In a large
bowl, combine cake mix, orange
soda and eggs. Stir to mix well.
Pour batter into prepared pan and
bake 20 to 30 minutes. Let cake
cool in pan for 15 minutes. Grease
a skewer or long-tined fork with
nonstick spray and poke holes into
top of warm cake. In a medium
bowl, combine orange gelatin
powder with 1 cup hot water; stir
until dissolved. Add 1 cup cold
water and stir. Pour entire gelatin
mixture over cake. Cover and
refrigerate for at least 2 hours.

Prepare Creamy Orange Frosting
(recipe on page 120) and frost cake.
Keep cake refrigerated until ready
to serve.

Orange Poppy Seed Cake

Makes 1 (10″) Bundt cake

Cake and Topping

1 (18.2 oz.) pkg. yellow cake mix

1 (3.4 oz.) pkg. vanilla instant pudding mix

½ C. vegetable oil

4 eggs

1 C. sour cream

½ C. orange juice

1½ tsp. almond extract

Grated peel of 1 orange, optional

¼ C. poppy seeds

Powdered sugar

Directions

Preheat oven to 350°. Grease and flour a 10″ Bundt or tube pan; set aside. In a large mixing bowl, stir together cake mix and pudding mix. Make a well in the center and pour in oil, eggs, sour cream, orange juice, almond extract and grated orange peel. Beat at low speed with electric mixer until blended. Scrape bowl and beat 2 additional minutes at medium speed. Stir in poppy seeds. Pour batter into prepared pan. Bake 50 minutes or until a toothpick inserted in center of cake comes out clean. Cool cake for 15 minutes in the pan. Remove cake from pan and sprinkle with powdered sugar before serving.

Variation

This cake can also be made substituting lemon juice and grated lemon peel for the orange juice and peel.

Cheesy Lemon Cake

Makes 1 (9 x 13″) cake

Cake and Topping

1 (18.2 oz.) pkg. lemon cake mix

Vegetable oil, eggs and water as directed on cake mix package

1 lb. ricotta cheese

Juice and grated peel of 1 lemon

¾ C. sugar

3 eggs

Powdered sugar

Directions

Preheat oven to 350°. Grease and flour a 9 x 13″ baking pan; set aside. In a large mixing bowl, combine cake mix, oil, eggs and water as directed on the cake mix package. Pour batter into prepared pan. In a separate bowl, mix ricotta cheese, lemon juice, grated lemon peel, sugar and eggs. Pour cheese mixture on top of cake batter. Bake 50 minutes. Cool cake completely and dust with powdered sugar

Lemon Blueberry Cake

Makes 1 (9 x 13″) cake

Cake and Toppings

1 (18.2 oz.) pkg. yellow cake mix

Vegetable oil, eggs and water as directed on cake mix package

1 T. grated lemon peel

2 C. fresh or frozen blueberries

1 (6 oz.) pkg. lemon gelatin powder

Powdered sugar

Whipped topping, optional

Directions

Preheat oven to 350°. Lightly grease a 9 x 13″ baking pan; set aside. In a large mixing bowl, combine cake mix, oil, eggs, and water as directed on the cake mix package. Stir in grated lemon peel. Pour batter into prepared pan. Sprinkle blueberries over batter. In a separate bowl, whisk together lemon gelatin powder and 1½ cups boiling water; stir until gelatin is dissolved. Slowly pour gelatin mixture over cake batter. Bake 33 to 38 minutes or until a toothpick inserted in center of cake comes out with moist crumbs. Cool cake in pan for 10 to 15 minutes.

Dust top of cake with powdered sugar. Invert pieces of cake on serving plates and serve cake warm with whipped topping, if desired. Refrigerate any leftover cake.

Raspberry Angel Food Cake

Makes 1 (10″) tube cake

Cake

1 (16 oz.) pkg. one-step angel food
  cake mix
½ tsp. almond extract
½ tsp. vanilla extract
1 (.3 oz.) pkg. sugar-free raspberry
  gelatin powder

Topping

1 (12 oz.) pkg. frozen unsweetened
  raspberries, thawed
1 T. sugar

Directions

Preheat oven as directed on cake
mix package. In a large mixing
bowl, prepare cake batter as
directed on cake mix package,
then fold in almond and vanilla
extracts. Spoon ⅔ of the batter
into an ungreased tube pan.
Add raspberry gelatin powder to
remaining batter in bowl and stir
to mix. Drop raspberry batter
by tablespoonfuls over batter
in pan. Use a knife to swirl the
batters. Bake according to package
directions. Immediately invert pan
onto a bottle or wire rack; cool
completely, about 1 hour. Carefully
run a knife around sides of pan to
remove cake. Cut into slices.

In a small bowl, combine
raspberries and sugar; serve
over cake

Dump-It-In Cake

Makes 1 (9 x 13″) square cake

Cake

1 (21 oz.) can cherry pie filling

½ C. crushed pineapple

1 (18.2 oz.) pkg. white or yellow cake mix

½ C. shredded coconut

½ C. chopped nuts

2 T. butter, cut into small pieces

Directions

Preheat oven to 375°. Thoroughly grease a 9 x 13″ baking pan. In order and into the prepared pan, evenly pour the cherry pie filling, pineapple, dry cake mix, coconut and nuts. Use a knife to stir through the mix lightly. Scatter pieces of butter evenly over the top of mixture. Bake 30 to 40 minutes or until a brown crust forms on top. Let cake cool in pan for 15 minutes, then serve warm.

Cream-Filled Twinkle Cake

Makes 1 (9 x 13″) cake

Cake

1 (18.2 oz.) pkg. yellow cake mix

Vegetable oil, eggs and water as
directed on cake mix package

Cooked Creamy Cupcake Filling

(recipe on page 126)

Directions

Preheat oven to 350°. Grease
and flour a 9 x 13″ baking pan;
set aside. In a large mixing bowl,
combine cake mix, oil, eggs, and
water as directed on the cake mix
package. Pour batter into prepared
pan and bake as directed. After
baking, cool cake 15 minutes in
pan, then turn cake out onto a
platter or foil-covered board which
has been sprinkled with powdered
sugar. Let cake cool completely.

Prepare Cooked Creamy Cupcake
Filling (recipe on page 126) and set
aside. With a long serrated knife,
carefully split cake into two layers.
Spread filling over bottom layer and
replace top layer. Cover with plastic
wrap and refrigerate overnight.
Let cake stand at least one day to
develop flavor before serving.

Root Beer Float Bundt Cake

Makes 1 (10˝) Bundt cake

Cake

1 (18.2 oz.) pkg. yellow cake mix
1 (12 oz.) can or bottle root beer
¼ C. vegetable oil
3 eggs

Glaze

1 to 1½ C. powdered sugar
6 T. root beer

Directions

Preheat oven to 350°. Grease and flour a 10″ Bundt pan. In a large bowl, stir together cake mix, 12 ounces root beer, oil and eggs until smooth. Pour batter into prepared pan. Bake 35 to 40 minutes or until a toothpick inserted in center of cake comes out clean. Cool cake in pan for 15 minutes, then invert onto a wire rack to cool completely.

With a skewer or long-tined fork, poke holes in top of cake about 2″ apart. In a small bowl, combine 1 cup powdered sugar and 6 tablespoons root beer; beat until smooth. Pour one coat of root beer glaze over cake, allowing it to soak into cake. After 15 minutes, thicken remaining glaze with additional powdered sugar and spread second coat on top like frosting, if desired.

Cakes from Scratch

Tips for Baking Cakes from Scratch

- If you use all-purpose flour, stated in this book as just "flour", in place of cake flour, remove 2 tablespoons of sifted flour from each measured cup. (1 cup sifted cake flour = 1 cup sifted all-purpose flour minus 2 tablespoons)

- When a recipe calls for a quantity of "sifted flour", sift it first and then measure it. When a recipe calls for a quantity of "flour, sifted", measure it first, then sift it together with other dry ingredients.

- For best results when beating egg whites, the bowl and beaters must be very clean, without any greasy residue. Use glass or metal bowls, not plastic or ceramic.

- If folding in beaten egg whites, do it gently to incorporate more air into the batter to produce a lighter cake.

- Use cake ingredients at room temperature whenever possible for best results.

White Cake with Citrus Filling

Cake

2 C. flour
1½ C. sugar
½ C. shortening
1 tsp. salt
⅔ C. plus ½ C. milk, divided
3½ tsp. baking powder
4 egg whites, whipped slightly
1 tsp. vanilla extract

Citrus Filling

(recipe on page 127)

White Frosting of choice

Directions

Preheat oven to 375°. Grease two 9″ round cake pans; set aside. In a large mixing bowl, combine flour, sugar, shortening, salt and ⅔ cup milk; beat 2 minutes with an electric mixer at medium speed. Stir in baking powder. Add remaining ½ cup milk, egg whites and vanilla extract; mix well. Pour equal amounts of batter into prepared pans and bake 25 to 30 minutes. Cool cakes in pans for 10 minutes then turn them out on a wire rack to cool completely.

Prepare Citrus Filling (recipe on page 127) and spread between the cake layers. Frost cake with white frosting of your choice. Refrigerate any leftover cake.

Orange-Lemon Cake

Makes 2 (9″) round layers

Cake

2 eggs, separated
1 tsp. cream of tartar
1½ C. sugar
2 C. plus 2 T. sifted flour
1 T. baking powder
1 tsp. salt
⅓ C. oil
1 C. milk, divided
1 tsp. vanilla extract
½ tsp. orange flavoring

Lemon Filling
(recipe on page 128)

Creamy Orange Frosting
(recipe on page 120)

Directions

Preheat oven to 350°. Grease and flour two 9″ baking pans; set aside. In a small mixing bowl, beat egg whites with electric mixer at high speed until frothy. Add cream of tartar; beat well. Gradually add ½ cup sugar, beating until stiff peaks form. In a separate bowl, stir together remaining 1 cup sugar, flour, baking powder and salt. Add oil, ¾ cup milk, vanilla extract and orange flavoring; beat 1 minute. Add remaining ¼ cup milk and both egg yolks; beat 1 minute. Gently fold in beaten egg whites. Spread batter evenly in prepared pans. Bake 25 to 30 minutes or until a toothpick inserted in center of cake comes out clean. Cool cake in pans for 10 minutes, then remove cake from pans and cool completely.

Prepare Lemon Filling (recipe on page 128) and spread between cake layers. Prepare Creamy Orange Frosting (recipe on page 120) or other frosting as desired, and frost entire cake. Refrigerate any leftover cake.

Cup o' Joe Apple Cake

Makes 1 (9 x 13″) cake

Cake

2 C. sugar

1 C. shortening

2 eggs

4 C. peeled, diced apples

2 tsp. vanilla extract

1 tsp. butter flavoring

3 C. sifted flour

2 tsp. ground cinnamon

2 tsp. baking soda

¾ tsp. salt

1 C. brewed coffee, cold

⅔ C. brown sugar

½ C. chopped nuts

Vanilla Glaze, optional
(recipe on page 123)

Directions

Preheat oven to 375°. Grease and flour a 9 x 13″ cake pan; set aside. In a large mixing bowl, use an electric mixer to cream together sugar and shortening; beat in eggs. Stir in diced apples, vanilla extract and butter flavoring. In a separate bowl, combine flour, cinnamon, baking soda and salt. Alternately add dry ingredients and coffee to creamed mixture, mixing well after each addition. Pour batter into prepared pan. Sprinkle brown sugar and chopped nuts evenly on top. Bake 40 to 50 minutes.

If desired, prepare Vanilla Glaze (recipe variation on page 123) and drizzle over cooled cake.

Oatmeal Applesauce Cake

Makes 1 (10˝) Bundt cake

Cake

1½ C. flour

1½ C. quick-cooking oats

¼ tsp. salt

1 T. baking powder

1½ tsp. ground cinnamon

1 tsp. ground nutmeg

¾ tsp. ground cloves

½ tsp. ground allspice

¾ C. butter, softened

1½ C. sugar

4 eggs

1 C. plus 2 T. applesauce

¾ C. milk

1½ C. raisins

1 C. coarsely chopped walnuts
or pecans

Frosting of choice, optional

Directions

Preheat oven to 350°. Grease and flour a 10˝ Bundt or tube pan; set aside. In a large bowl, mix flour, oats, salt, baking powder, cinnamon, nutmeg, cloves and allspice; set aside. In a large mixing bowl, use an electric mixer to cream together butter and sugar. Beat in eggs. Add applesauce and milk; beat well. Add flour mixture; mix well. Stir in raisins and walnuts. Spread batter in prepared pan and bake 55 to 65 minutes or until a toothpick inserted in center of cake comes out clean. Cool cake in pan for 15 minutes, then invert on wire rack to cool. Serve cool or warm.

Frost as desired. Refrigerate any leftover cake. This cake packs well for picnics and camping.

Nutty Apple Cake

Makes 1 (10 x 15˝) jelly roll cake

Cake

¾ C. butter or margarine, softened
1 C. sugar
½ C. brown sugar
2 eggs
1 C. buttermilk
2½ C. flour
1 tsp. baking soda
1 tsp. baking powder
1 tsp. ground cinnamon
½ tsp. salt
2 C. peeled, diced apples

Topping

¾ C. sugar
1 tsp. ground cinnamon
½ C. chopped nuts

Vanilla Glaze, optional
(recipe on page 123)

Directions

Preheat oven to 350°. Grease a 10 x 15″ jelly roll pan; set aside. In a large mixing bowl, use an electric mixer to cream together butter, sugar and brown sugar. Add eggs and buttermilk; mix well. In a separate bowl, stir together flour, baking soda, baking powder, cinnamon and salt. Add flour mixture to creamed mixture; mix until well blended. Stir in diced apples. Pour batter into prepared pan.

Prepare topping by combining sugar, cinnamon and chopped nuts in a small bowl. Sprinkle topping over cake batter and bake 25 to 30 minutes. Cool cake in pan.

Prepare Vanilla Glaze (recipe variation on page 123) and drizzle over cake, if desired. Refrigerate any leftover cake.

Raspberry Swirl Cake

Makes 1 (10″) tube cake

Cake

1 C. plus 1 T. butter or
   margarine, softened
2 C. sugar
3 C. sifted flour
4 tsp. baking powder
1 tsp. salt
1⅓ C. milk
2 tsp. vanilla extract
6 egg whites, room temperature
Pinch of salt
½ C. raspberry jelly
Red food coloring

Glaze Options

Raspberry jam, strained or
   Almond or Vanilla Glaze
   (recipes on page 123)

Directions

Preheat oven to 350°. Grease and
flour a 9″ or 10″ tube pan. In a
large mixing bowl, use an electric
mixer to cream together butter and
sugar until light and fluffy. In a
separate bowl, stir together sifted
flour, baking powder and salt. Add
flour mixture alternately with milk
to creamed mixture, beginning and
ending with dry ingredients. Stir
in vanilla extract. In a small mixing
bowl, combine egg whites with
a pinch of salt; beat egg whites until
stiff peaks form. Gently fold egg
whites into batter with a spoon.
In a small saucepan over low heat,
warm jelly until melted; cool slightly.
Stir 1 cup of cake batter into jelly;
mix well. Add a few drops of food
coloring to give desired pink color;
set aside. Spread white batter into
prepared pan and pour pink batter
on top. With a spoon, swirl pink
batter into white batter as desired.
Bake 50 to 55 minutes; cool for 10
minutes, then turn out on wire rack
or serving plate to cool completely.

Drizzle with warmed, strained
raspberry jam, or prepare Almond
or Vanilla Glaze (recipes on
page 123) and drizzle over cake.
Refrigerate any leftover cake.

Cranberry Cake

Makes 1 (10˝) Bundt cake

Cake

½ C. butter, softened

1 C. sugar

2 eggs

1 (8 oz.) carton sour cream

1 tsp. almond extract

2 C. flour

1½ tsp. baking powder

½ tsp. baking soda

½ tsp. salt

1 (16 oz.) can whole cranberry
   sauce

Almond Glaze

(recipe on page 123)

Directions

Preheat oven to 350°. Spray a Bundt pan with nonstick cooking spray; set aside. In a large mixing bowl, use an electric mixer to cream together butter and sugar. Add eggs and beat well. Add sour cream and almond extract; mix well. In a separate bowl, mix flour, baking powder, baking soda and salt. Add flour mixture to creamed mixture and beat until smooth. Pour half the batter into prepared Bundt pan. Spoon half the cranberry sauce over batter in pan. Cover with remaining batter. Top with remaining cranberry sauce. (It sinks in during baking.) Bake 50 to 60 minutes. Cool cake in pan for 15 minutes, then invert onto a serving plate to cool completely.

Prepare Almond Glaze (recipe on page 123) and drizzle over cake. Refrigerate any leftover cake.

Banana-Walnut Cake

Makes 1 (9 x 13˝) cake or 2 (9˝) layers

Cake

⅔ C. butter, softened

1½ C. sugar

2 eggs

1 C. mashed bananas

¼ tsp. black walnut flavoring

¼ tsp. banana flavoring

¼ C. buttermilk

2 C. sifted flour

1 tsp. baking soda

½ tsp. salt

½ C. chopped walnuts

Cream Cheese Frosting
(recipe on page 122) or
Vanilla Buttercream Frosting
(recipe on page 113)

Directions

Preheat oven to 350°. Grease and flour a 9 x 13″ baking pan. In a large mixing bowl, use an electric mixer to cream together butter and sugar until light and fluffy. Add eggs, one at a time, beating well after each addition. Add mashed bananas, walnut and banana flavorings and buttermilk; stir well. In a separate bowl, combine flour, baking soda and salt; mix well. Add flour mixture to batter, mixing well. Stir in chopped walnuts. Pour batter into prepared pan and bake 28 to 35 minutes or until a toothpick inserted in center of cake comes out clean. Cool cake completely.

Frost cake with prepared Cream Cheese Frosting (recipe on page 122) or Vanilla Buttercream Frosting (recipe on page 113). Refrigerate any leftover cake.

Fresh Cherry Cake

Makes 1 (9″) springform cake

Cake and Topping

1 lb. fresh cherries, cleaned
  and pitted
2 eggs
¾ C. sugar
½ C. butter, melted and cooled
⅓ C. milk
1 tsp. vanilla extract
Zest of 1 lemon
1½ C. flour
1½ tsp. baking powder
¼ tsp. salt
Whipped cream, optional

Directions

Preheat oven to 400°. Grease and flour a 9″ springform pan; line bottom of pan with parchment paper and set aside. Cut 15 cherries in half; set aside for garnishing. Leave remaining cherries whole; set aside. In a large mixing bowl, use an electric mixer to beat together eggs and sugar for 3 to 5 minutes or until thick and creamy. Add melted butter, milk, vanilla extract and lemon zest; beat until well blended. In a separate bowl, combine flour, baking powder and salt. Add flour mixture to creamed mixture; stir until moistened. Gently fold in the whole pitted cherries. Pour batter into prepared pan, smoothing top with a spatula. Bake 15 minutes, then remove from oven. Quickly arrange remaining cherry halves on top of cake, cut side down. Return cake to oven and bake 20 additional minutes or until golden brown and a toothpick inserted in center of cake comes out clean. Cool cake in pan for 10 minutes, then turn out onto a serving plate. Serve cake warm or at room temperature with whipped cream. Refrigerate any leftover cake.

Buttermilk Nutmeg Cake

Makes 1 (9 x 13″) cake

Cake

½ C. shortening
1½ C. sugar
3 eggs
½ tsp. vanilla extract
½ tsp. butter flavoring
2 C. sifted flour
1 tsp. baking powder
1 tsp. baking soda
2 tsp. ground nutmeg
½ tsp. salt
1 C. buttermilk

Caramel Frosting
(recipe on page 115) or
Broiled Coconut Topping
(recipe on page 121)

Directions

Preheat oven to 350°. Grease and flour a 9 x 13″ baking pan; set aside. In a large mixing bowl, use an electric mixer to cream together shortening and sugar. Add eggs, one at a time, beating well after each addition. Add vanilla extract and butter flavoring; beat well. In a separate bowl, sift together flour, baking powder, baking soda, nutmeg and salt. Alternately add flour mixture and buttermilk to creamed mixture, beating well after each addition. Spread batter in prepared pan and bake 35 to 40 minutes or until a toothpick inserted in center of cake comes out clean. Cool cake 30 minutes.

Frost cake with prepared Caramel Frosting (recipe on page 115) or a double recipe of Broiled Coconut Topping (recipe on page 121). Refrigerate any leftover cake.

Easy White Cake

Cake

1 C. sugar
½ C. butter, softened
2 eggs
2 tsp. vanilla extract
1½ C. flour
1¾ tsp. baking powder
½ C. milk

Frosting of choice, optional

Directions

Preheat oven to 350°. Grease and flour a 9˝ square baking pan. In a medium bowl, use an electric mixer to cream together sugar and butter. Beat in eggs, one at a time. Add vanilla extract and mix well. In a separate bowl, combine flour and baking powder. Add flour mixture to creamed mixture and blend well. Add milk and mix until batter is smooth. Pour batter into prepared pan. Bake 30 to 40 minutes or until cake springs back when touched. Frost as desired. Refrigerate any leftover cake.

Traditional Yellow Layer Cake

Makes 2 (9″) round layers

Cake

½ C. butter or margarine, softened

1⅔ C. sugar

1 T. vanilla extract

3 eggs

2¼ C. flour

2¼ tsp. baking powder

½ tsp. salt

1¼ C. skim milk

German Chocolate Frosting

(recipe on page 121) or other frosting of your choice

Directions

Preheat oven to 350°. Coat bottoms of two 9″ round cake pans with cooking spray. Line pan bottoms with waxed paper and coat with cooking spray, then dust with flour; set aside. In a large mixing bowl, use an electric mixer at medium speed to cream together butter, sugar and vanilla extract until smooth and fluffy. Add eggs, one at a time, beating well after each addition. In a separate bowl, combine flour, baking powder and salt; stir to mix well. Alternately add flour mixture and milk to creamed mixture, beginning and ending with flour mixture. Pour batter into prepared pans. Bake 30 minutes or until a toothpick inserted in center of cake comes out clean. Cool cake in pans for 10 minutes, then remove cake from pans, remove waxed paper and cool completely.

Prepare German Chocolate Frosting (recipe on page 121). Spread ½ cup of frosting between cake layers and use remaining frosting to frost cake. Refrigerate any leftover cake.

Sour Cream Chocolate Cake

Makes 3 (9˝) round layers

Cake

1 C. unsweetened cocoa powder
1 C. butter, softened
2½ C. sugar
4 eggs
2 tsp. vanilla extract
3 C. cake flour
2 tsp. baking soda
½ tsp. baking powder
½ tsp. salt
1 C. sour cream

Sour Cream Chocolate Frosting
(recipe on page 116)

Directions

Preheat oven to 350°. Grease and flour three 9″ round baking pans. Line the bottom of each pan with parchment or waxed paper; set aside. Dissolve cocoa powder in 1 cup boiling water; set aside to cool. In a large mixing bowl, use an electric mixer to cream together butter and sugar. Add eggs, one at a time, beating well after each addition. Add vanilla extract and mix until blended. In a separate bowl, combine flour, baking soda, baking powder and salt. Alternately add flour mixture, cocoa mixture and sour cream to creamed mixture; blend well. Pour an equal amount of batter into prepared pans. Bake 30 to 35 minutes or until a toothpick inserted in center of cake comes out clean. Cool cake in pans for 10 minutes, then remove from pans and remove parchment paper to cool completely.

Prepare and spread Sour Cream Chocolate Frosting (recipe on page 116) between layers and over cake. Refrigerate any leftover cake.

Old-Fashioned Chocolate Cake

Makes 1 (9 x 13″) cake or 2 (9″) layers

Cake

½ C. unsweetened cocoa powder

½ C. shortening

1½ C. sugar

3 eggs, separated

1 tsp. vanilla extract

1½ C. flour

½ tsp. salt

1 tsp. baking soda

1 tsp. baking powder

Pinch of salt

Frosting of choice, optional

Directions

Preheat oven to 350°. Grease and flour a 9 x 13″ baking pan; set aside. In a small bowl, mix cocoa powder with ½ cup boiling water. Stir until well mixed; set aside to cool. In a large mixing bowl, use an electric mixer to cream together shortening and sugar. In a small bowl, beat 3 egg yolks. Add beaten egg yolks, ½ cup cold water and vanilla extract to creamed mixture; mix well. Add cocoa mixture; mix well. In a separate bowl, combine flour, ½ teaspoon salt, baking soda and baking powder; mix until well blended. Add flour mixture to creamed mixture and stir. With an electric mixer, beat 3 egg whites and a pinch of salt until stiff peaks form. Fold egg whites into cake batter just until blended. Spread batter in prepared pan and bake 30 to 40 minutes or until a toothpick inserted in center of cake comes out clean. Frost as desired.

Cola Cake

Cake

2 C. flour
2 C. sugar
1 C. butter
3 T. unsweetened cocoa powder
1 C. cola
½ C. buttermilk
2 eggs, beaten
1 tsp. baking soda
1 tsp. vanilla extract
1½ C. miniature marshmallows

Cola Icing

(recipe on page 120)

Directions

Preheat oven to 350°. Grease a 9 x 13˝ baking pan; set aside. In a large mixing bowl, combine flour and sugar; set aside. In a small saucepan over medium heat, combine butter, cocoa powder and cola; bring mixture to a boil. Remove from heat and pour butter mixture over flour and sugar in bowl. Beat with an electric mixer at low speed until well blended. Add buttermilk, eggs, baking soda, vanilla extract and marshmallows. Beat thoroughly at medium speed. Batter will be thin and marshmallows will float on top. Pour batter into prepared pan. Bake 30 to 35 minutes. Let cake cool for 10 minutes.

Prepare and frost cake with Cola Icing (recipe on page 120) or icing of your choice. Refrigerate any leftover cake.

Moist Chocolate Zucchini Cake

Makes 1 (10″) Bundt cake

Cake

¾ C. sugar

½ C. brown sugar

½ C. fat-free cream cheese, softened

⅓ C. vegetable oil

2 eggs

2 egg whites

1 tsp. vanilla extract

2½ C. flour

½ C. unsweetened cocoa powder

2 tsp. baking powder

½ tsp baking soda

½ tsp. salt

½ tsp. ground cinnamon

¾ C. fat-free buttermilk

2 C. shredded zucchini

⅔ C. semi-sweet chocolate chips

¼ C. chopped walnuts

Chocolate Glaze
(recipe on page 124) or
Baker's Frosting
(recipe on page 112)

Directions

Preheat oven to 350°. Generously grease and flour a 10″ Bundt pan; set aside. In a large mixing bowl, combine sugar, brown sugar, cream cheese and oil; beat with an electric mixer at medium speed about 5 minutes or until well blended. Add eggs and egg whites, one at a time, beating well after each addition. Beat in vanilla extract. In a separate bowl, combine flour, cocoa powder, baking powder, baking soda, salt and cinnamon; mix well. Alternately add flour mixture and buttermilk to creamed mixture, beginning and ending with flour mixture and blending well after each addition. Stir in zucchini, chocolate chips and walnuts. Pour batter into prepared pan and bake 50 to 60 minutes or until a toothpick inserted in center of cake comes out clean. Cool cake in pan 10 minutes. Remove from pan and cool completely on wire rack.

Prepare Chocolate Glaze (recipe on page 124) or Baker's Frosting (recipe on page 112) thinning it slightly with warm water to a drizzling consistency. Drizzle over cake. Refrigerate any leftover cake.

Easy Yellow Snack Cake

Makes 1 (8˝) square cake

Cake

¼ C. butter or margarine, softened
⅔ C. sugar
1 egg
1 tsp. vanilla extract
1½ C. flour
2 tsp. baking powder
¼ tsp. salt
¾ C. milk

Broiled Coconut Topping

(recipe on page 121)

Directions

Preheat oven to 350°. Grease an 8″ square baking pan; set aside. In a medium mixing bowl, use an electric mixer to cream together butter and sugar. Beat in egg and vanilla extract. In a separate bowl, combine flour, baking powder and salt. Alternately add flour mixture and milk to creamed mixture, beating after each addition. Pour batter into prepared pan and bake 30 minutes or until a toothpick inserted in center of cake comes out clean. Cool cake slightly.

Prepare Broiled Coconut Topping (recipe on page 121), spread on cake and broil as directed. Serve cake warm. Refrigerate any leftover cake.

Low-Fat Chocolate Cake page 23

Great cakes...

Filled Sour Cream Coffee Cakes page 17

Banana Buttermilk Cupcakes page 94

Chocolate Chip Icing page 117

Vanilla Cupcakes page 83
with Buttercream Icing page 113
and Royal Icing flowers page 111

for any season...

Traditional Strawberry Shortcake
page 76

Classic Pound Cake
page 69

Old Fashioned Chocolate Cake page 61
German Chocolate Frosting page 121

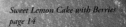
Sweet Lemon Cake with Berries
page 14

and any reason.

Party Pumpkin Roll
page 78

Lemon Blueberry Cake page 42

Cola Cake page 62

67

Raspberry Swirl Cake
page 53

Bake, Take & Celebrate!

Malt & Mocha Cupcakes
page 87

Moist Chocolate
Zuchini Cake page 63

Classic Carrot Cake
page 75

68

Classic Pound Cake

Makes 1 (9 x 5˝) loaf cake

Cake

1 C. butter, softened

1 C. sugar

4 eggs, divided

¼ tsp. salt

Pinch of ground mace or nutmeg

1 T. vanilla extract

½ tsp. lemon flavoring

¼ C. milk

2 C. cake flour

1 tsp. baking powder

Fruit or chocolate sauce, optional

Directions

Preheat oven to 325°. Grease the bottom of a 9 x 5″ loaf pan. Line bottom of pan with parchment or waxed paper; set aside. In a large mixing bowl, use an electric mixer to cream together butter and sugar until soft and fluffy. Add 3 eggs, one at a time, and beat after each addition. Add salt, mace, vanilla extract and lemon flavoring; beat well. In a measuring cup, mix remaining egg with milk until well blended; set aside. In a separate bowl, sift together flour and baking powder. Alternately add flour mixture and milk mixture to creamed mixture, beginning and ending with flour mixture, beating at low speed until well blended. Spread batter in prepared pan. Bake 50 to 60 minutes or until surface is cracked and a thin knife inserted in thickest part of cake comes out clean. Cool cake in pan for 10 minutes, then turn out of pan onto wire rack; remove parchment paper before cooling completely. Refrigerate cake. Best if served the next day with fruit or chocolate sauce.

Sensational Strawberry Yogurt Pound Cake

Makes 1 (9 x 5″) loaf cake

Cake

½ C. butter, softened

1 C. sugar

4 eggs

1 (6 oz.) carton nonfat
strawberry yogurt

¼ tsp. almond extract

2 C. flour

2 tsp. baking powder

½ tsp. salt

Almond or **Vanilla Glaze**,
(recipes on page 123)

Directions

Preheat oven to 325°. Grease and
flour a 9 x 5″ loaf pan; set aside.
In a large mixing bowl, use an
electric mixer at medium speed to
cream together butter and sugar
until light and fluffy. Beat in eggs,
yogurt and almond extract until
well blended. In a separate bowl,
combine flour, baking powder and
salt. Add flour mixture to creamed
mixture, ½ cup at a time, and beat
at low speed until blended. Spread
batter evenly in prepared pan and
bake 60 to 70 minutes or until a
thin knife inserted in thickest part
of cake comes out clean. Cool cake
in pan for 10 minutes, then remove
cake from pan and cool completely.

Prepare Almond or Vanilla
Glaze (recipes on page 123)
and drizzle over cake. Refrigerate
any leftover cake.

Traditional Angel Food Cake

Makes 1 (10˝) tube cake

Cake

1 C. sifted cake flour
1½ C. sugar, divided
12 egg whites, room temperature
2 pinches of salt, divided
1 tsp. cream of tartar
1½ tsp. fresh lemon juice
1½ tsp. vanilla extract
½ tsp. almond extract

Chocolate Glaze

(recipe on page 124)

Directions

Preheat oven to 325°. In a medium bowl, combine flour and ¾ cup sugar, stirring with a whisk. In a large mixing bowl, combine egg whites with a pinch of salt. Beat with electric mixer at high speed until foamy. Add cream of tartar and another pinch of salt; beat until soft peaks form. Beat in remaining ¾ cup sugar, 2 tablespoons at a time, until stiff peaks form. Beat in lemon juice, vanilla and almond extract. Sift ¼ cup flour mixture over egg white mixture and fold in gently. Repeat with remaining flour mixture, ¼ cup at a time. Spread batter evenly in an ungreased 10˝ tube pan. Cut through batter with a knife to break any air pockets. Bake 50 to 60 minutes or until cake springs back when lightly touched. Invert cake in pan over a bottle and cool completely. Loosen cake from sides of pan and tube using a narrow metal spatula. Invert cake onto a platter and remove tube.

Prepare Chocolate Glaze (recipe on page 124) or other glaze of your choice and drizzle over cake.

Super Sponge Cake

Makes 1 (10˝) tube cake

Cake

4 eggs, separated
1½ C. sugar, divided
1⅔ C. cake flour
½ tsp. baking powder
1 tsp. cream of tartar, divided
⅛ tsp. salt
1 tsp. lemon flavoring
1 tsp. vanilla extract

7-Minute White Icing
(recipe on page 112) or
Lemon Glaze
(recipe on page 124)

Directions

Preheat oven to 325°. Separate eggs and place yolks into a medium bowl; set whites aside. Beat yolks with an electric mixer until thick and creamy. Add 1 cup sugar and 2 teaspoons cold water; beat well. In a separate bowl, sift together cake flour, baking powder, ½ teaspoon cream of tartar and salt, sifting 4 to 5 times. Alternately add flour mixture and ½ cup hot water to egg mixture, mixing well after each addition. In a large mixing bowl, beat reserved egg whites with remaining ½ teaspoon cream of tartar until foamy. Gradually add remaining ½ cup sugar, beating to stiff peaks. Gently stir in lemon flavoring and vanilla extract. Fold beaten egg whites into cake batter. Spread batter in ungreased 10˝ tube pan. Bake about 55 minutes or until cake springs back when lightly touched. Invert cake in pan over a bottle and cool completely. Loosen cake from edges of pan with a long knife or flexible spatula. Invert on a serving plate and remove tube.

Prepare and frost cake with 7-Minute White Icing (recipe on page 112), Lemon Glaze (recipe on page 124), or other frosting of your choice.

Orange and Lemon Chiffon Cake

Makes 1 (10″) tube cake

Cake

2¼ C. sifted cake flour

1½ C. sugar

1 T. baking powder

1 tsp. salt

½ C. vegetable oil

5 egg yolks, room temperature

1 T. grated orange peel

2 tsp. grated lemon peel

¾ C. fresh orange juice

8 egg whites, room temperature

Pinch of salt

½ tsp. cream of tartar

Lemon or Orange Glaze
(recipes on page 124) or

Creamy Orange Frosting
(recipe on page 120)

Directions

Preheat oven to 325°. In a large bowl, sift together flour, sugar, baking powder and 1 teaspoon salt. Make a well in the center; add oil, egg yolks, orange peel, lemon peel and orange juice. Whisk until smooth; set aside. In a large mixing bowl, use an electric mixer at medium speed to beat egg whites with a pinch of salt until frothy. Add cream of tartar and beat at high speed until stiff peaks form. Gradually add yolk mixture in a thin steady stream into beaten egg whites, folding them into whites gently with a rubber scraper. Pour batter into ungreased 10″ tube pan. Bake 55 to 60 minutes or until a toothpick inserted in center of cake comes out clean and cake springs back when lightly touched. Immediately invert pan onto the neck of a funnel or bottle. Let cake hang upside down until completely cool, about 3 hours. Loosen cake from sides of pan and tube using a narrow metal spatula. Remove cake and turn upright onto serving plate.

Prepare Lemon or Orange Glaze (recipes on page 124) and drizzle on cake, or prepare Creamy Orange Frosting (recipe on page 120) and spread on cake.

Lemon Poppy Seed Cake

Makes 1 (9 x 5″) loaf

Cake

2¼ C. cake flour

1 C. plus 2 T. sugar, divided

1 tsp. salt

1½ T. grated lemon peel

¼ C. poppy seeds

1⅓ C. butter, softened

5 eggs

Syrup Topping

¾ C. sugar

¾ C. lemon juice

Directions

Preheat oven to 350°. Grease and flour a 9 x 5″ loaf pan; set aside. In a large bowl, sift together flour, 1 cup plus 2 tablespoons sugar and salt. Mix in lemon peel, poppy seeds and butter. Add eggs, one at a time, beating well after each addition. Pour batter into prepared pan. Bake 60 to 70 minutes or until a toothpick inserted in center of cake comes out clean.

In a small saucepan over low heat, combine ¾ cup sugar with lemon juice. Cook and stir until sugar is dissolved; cool to room temperature. After removing cake from oven, poke top of cake many times with a toothpick. Pour lemon syrup over warm cake, letting syrup soak in as cake cools for 15 minutes. Remove cake from pan to cool completely. Wrap cooled cake in foil or plastic wrap and let it stand overnight. Best if served the next day.

Classic Carrot Cake

Makes 2 (8˝ or 9˝) round layers

Cake

2 C. flour

1 tsp. baking soda

1½ tsp. baking powder

1 tsp. salt

2 tsp. ground cinnamon

4 eggs

1½ C. sugar

1 C. vegetable oil

2 tsp. vanilla extract

1 (8 oz.) can crushed pineapple,
   drained

2½ C. finely grated carrots

1 C. chopped nuts

1 C. flaked coconut, optional

Cream Cheese Frosting

(recipe on page 122)

Directions

Preheat oven to 350°. Spray two 8˝ or 9˝ round baking pans with nonstick baking spray. Line the bottoms of pans with a circle of parchment paper; set aside. In a large bowl, stir together flour, baking soda, baking powder, salt and cinnamon; set aside. In a large mixing bowl, use an electric mixer to beat eggs until frothy. Gradually add sugar and beat for 3 to 4 minutes or until batter is thick and light yellow. Add oil in a steady stream, beating constantly. Beat in vanilla extract and pineapple. Add flour mixture and beat until well mixed. With a large spoon, fold in grated carrots, nuts and coconut until well blended. Divide batter evenly and spread in prepared pans. Bake 25 to 35 minutes or until a toothpick inserted in center of cakes comes out clean. Cool cakes in pan for 10 minutes, then invert onto wire rack and remove parchment paper to cool completely.

Prepare a double recipe of Cream Cheese Frosting, using 8 ounces of cream cheese instead of 6 ounces (recipe on page 122). Place 1 cake layer, top side down, on a serving platter. Spread about ⅓ of frosting on cake. Place other cake layer on top of frosting, top side facing up. Spread remaining frosting over the top and sides of cake. Refrigerate any leftover cake.

Traditional Strawberry Shortcake

Makes 1 (8″) round cake

Cake

2¼ C. flour

2 tsp. baking powder

¼ C. sugar

¼ tsp. salt

⅓ C. butter or shortening

1 egg, beaten

⅔ C. milk

1 tsp. vanilla extract

Toppings

Butter, optional

Sliced strawberries, sugared

Whipped cream or whipped topping

Directions

Preheat oven to 425°. Grease and flour an 8″ round cake pan; set aside. In a medium bowl, combine flour, baking powder, sugar and salt. With a pastry blender or two knives, cut in the butter until mixture resembles coarse crumbs. Make a well in the center and add beaten egg, milk and vanilla extract. Stir until just combined. Spread batter in prepared pan and bake 15 to 20 minutes or until golden brown. Let cool 10 minutes in pan, then remove from pan.

Cut partially cooled cake into wedges like a pie. Slice each shortcake wedge in half horizontally to make layers. Spread layers with softened butter, if desired. Spoon sweetened strawberries between the two layers of shortcake, then top with more berries and whipped cream. Refrigerate any leftover cake.

Victorian Bundt Cake

Makes 1 (10˝) Bundt cake

Cake and Topping

3 C. flour

2 C. sugar

1 tsp. ground cinnamon

1 tsp. baking soda

½ tsp. salt

1 (8 oz.) can crushed pineapple with juice

1 C. vegetable oil

3 eggs, well-beaten

3 medium bananas, peeled and chopped

1 C. finely chopped walnuts or pecans

½ tsp. vanilla extract

1 T. butter, melted

1 C. powdered sugar

Directions

Preheat oven to 325°. Grease a 10˝ Bundt pan; set aside. In a large bowl, combine flour, sugar, cinnamon, baking soda and salt; mix well and set aside. Remove 2 tablespoons of pineapple juice and set aside for the glaze. Add the remaining pineapple and juice, oil, eggs, bananas, nuts and vanilla extract to flour mixture; stir until well blended but do not beat. Pour batter into prepared pan and bake 60 to 70 minutes or until a toothpick inserted in center of cake comes out clean. Cool cake in pan for 10 minutes before inverting cake onto wire rack to cool completely.

In a small bowl, combine reserved pineapple juice, melted butter and powdered sugar; mix well. Drizzle mixture over cooled cake. If preferred, frost with Cream Cheese Frosting (recipe on page 122) instead.

Party Pumpkin Roll

Makes 1 (10 x 15˝) jelly roll cake

Cake

¾ C. flour
1 tsp. baking powder
2 tsp. ground cinnamon
1 tsp. ground ginger
½ tsp. ground nutmeg
½ tsp. salt
3 eggs
1 C. sugar
⅔ C. canned pumpkin
1 tsp. lemon juice
Chopped walnuts, optional
Powdered sugar

Cream Cheese Filling
(recipe on page 127)

Directions

Preheat oven to 350°. Line a 10 x 15˝ jelly roll pan with parchment or waxed paper, then grease it and dust lightly with flour; set aside. In a small bowl, combine flour, baking powder, cinnamon, ginger, nutmeg and salt; set aside. In a large mixing bowl, use an electric mixer to beat eggs and sugar for 5 minutes or until fluffy and light yellow. Add pumpkin and lemon juice; stir gently until well blended. Add flour mixture to pumpkin mixture; stir until combined. Spread batter evenly in prepared pan. If desired, sprinkle chopped walnuts on top of batter. Bake 15 minutes or until cake springs back when lightly touched. Remove from oven and cool cake in pan for 10 minutes. Sift some powdered sugar evenly onto a clean kitchen towel. Invert cake onto towel and gently roll up cake and towel starting with the short end. Cool cake completely.

Prepare Cream Cheese Filling (recipe on page 127). Carefully unroll cake and spread filling over cake. Gently roll cake up again, ending with seam side down. Cover cake roll with waxed or parchment paper and refrigerate or freeze at least 1 hour. Slice and serve cold. Refrigerate any leftover cake.

Rhubarb Cake with Topping

Makes 1 (9 x 13″) cake

Cake and Toppings

⅔ C. shortening

2½ C. sugar, divided

2 eggs

1 C. brewed coffee, cold

3 C. flour

2 tsp. baking soda

½ tsp. salt

4 tsp. ground cinnamon, divided

½ tsp. ground cloves

½ tsp. ground nutmeg

2 C. chopped rhubarb

1 C. chopped walnuts

1 C. raisins, optional

Whipped topping, optional

Directions

Preheat oven to 350°. Grease a 9 x 13″ baking pan; set aside. In a large mixing bowl, use an electric mixer to cream together shortening and 2 cups sugar. Add eggs and beat well. Stir in cold coffee. In a separate bowl, combine flour, baking soda, salt, 2 teaspoons cinnamon, cloves and nutmeg; mix well. Add dry ingredients to creamed mixture and blend well. Stir in rhubarb, walnuts and raisins. Spread cake batter in prepared pan. In a small bowl, mix remaining ½ cup sugar and remaining 2 teaspoons cinnamon. Sprinkle on top of cake batter before baking. Bake 40 to 50 minutes or until cake springs back when lightly touched. Cool cake in the pan before cutting. Place a dollop of whipped topping on each piece, if desired.

Peach Upside-Down Cake

Cake

¼ C. butter, softened

½ C. brown sugar

1½ C. canned peach slices, drained

6 maraschino cherries, halved

⅓ C. shortening

½ C. sugar

1 egg

1¼ C. sifted cake flour

1½ tsp. baking powder

1½ tsp. salt

½ tsp. grated orange peel

½ C. orange juice

Directions

Preheat oven to 350°. In the bottom of an 8˝ round cake pan, spread softened butter; sprinkle with brown sugar. Arrange peaches and cherries, cut side up, on brown sugar. In a large mixing bowl, use an electric mixer to cream together shortening and sugar. Add egg; beat well. In a separate bowl, sift together flour, baking powder and salt; set aside. In a measuring cup, combine orange peel with orange juice; set aside. Alternately add flour mixture and orange juice mixture to creamed mixture, beating well after each addition. Pour batter over peaches and cherries in pan, without disturbing fruit. Bake 45 to 50 minutes or until a toothpick inserted in center of cake comes out clean. Cool cake in pan for 10 minutes, then invert cake on serving plate and remove pan.

Cupcakes

Tips for Baking Cupcakes

• Most cake recipes can be prepared and then baked in muffin pans to create cupcakes. Bake the cupcakes at the same temperature as directed for a 9 x 13″ cake, but shorten baking time and check degree of doneness with a toothpick after 15 minutes.

• Place paper liners in muffin pans or grease each cup in the pan before adding batter.

• Do not overfill cups with batter. To prevent spillover or a crown from forming, fill cups approximately ⅔ to ¾ full unless directed otherwise in recipe.

• Cool cupcakes completely before frosting them.

• Bake and freeze unfrosted cupcakes several weeks before a party. Remove them from the freezer, frost and decorate them just before the party.

Cupcakes in Ice Cream Cones

Makes 30 to 36 cupcakes

Cupcakes

1 (18.2 oz.) pkg. chocolate cake mix (or flavor of your choice)

Vegetable oil, eggs and water as directed on cake mix package

30 to 36 flat-bottomed ice cream cones

Frosting of choice

Directions

Preheat oven to 350°. In a large mixing bowl, combine cake mix with oil, eggs and water as directed on the cake mix package; mix well. Fill each cone about half full with batter, filling only those cones your muffin pan can hold. Stand cones upright in the muffin pan. Bake 20 to 30 minutes. Cool completely before frosting, about 1 hour. Leftover batter should be refrigerated until ready to fill and bake remaining cones. Frost and decorate cupcakes as desired.

Tip

If no muffin tin is available, a tube pan can be used to hold cones. Cover pan's opening with heavy-duty aluminum foil and poke evenly spaced holes around pan. Place a cone in each hole so cones stand up during baking.

Vanilla Cupcakes

Makes 12 large or 48 miniature cupcakes

Cupcakes

1½ C. plus 1 T. flour
1½ tsp. baking powder
¼ tsp. salt
½ C. plus 1 T. butter, softened
¾ C. sugar
1 egg
2 egg yolks
1½ tsp. vanilla extract
½ C. plus 1 T. whipping cream

Buttercream Icing
(recipe on page 113)

Royal Icing
(recipe on page 111)
Food coloring, optional

Directions

Preheat oven to 350°. Place paper liners in muffin pans. In a small bowl, mix together flour, baking powder and salt; set aside. In a large mixing bowl, beat butter with electric mixer at high speed until creamy. Add sugar, egg, egg yolks, vanilla extract and whipping cream; beat until well blended. Reduce mixer speed to low and add flour mixture, beating until just combined. Pour batter evenly into cupcake liners, filling each cup about ¾ full and smoothing tops with back of spoon. Bake 22 to 24 minutes or until cupcakes are lightly golden and spring back when gently touched. (Bake miniature cupcakes about 15 to 18 minutes.) Cool cupcakes for 5 minutes in the pan, then remove them to a wire rack to finish cooling.

Prepare Buttercream Icing (recipe on page 113) and tint with food coloring as desired. Spread or pipe generously on cupcakes. Prepare and tint Royal Icing (recipe on page 111). Use a decorator's tube to pipe on flower shapes or other designs. Refrigerate any leftover cupcakes.

Yummy Chocolate Cupcakes

Makes 24 to 30 cupcakes

Cupcakes

1⅓ C. flour

2 tsp. baking powder

¼ tsp. baking soda

¾ C. unsweetened cocoa powder

⅛ tsp. salt

3 T. butter, softened

1½ C. sugar

2 eggs

¾ tsp. vanilla extract

1 C. milk

Frosting of choice

Directions

Preheat oven to 350°. Place paper liners in muffin pans. In a medium bowl, sift together flour, baking powder, baking soda, cocoa powder and salt; set aside. In a large mixing bowl, use an electric mixer to cream together butter and sugar until fluffy. Add the eggs, one at a time, and beat well with each addition. Stir in vanilla extract. Alternately add flour mixture and milk to creamed mixture; beat well.

Pour batter evenly into cupcake liners, filling each cup about ⅔ full. Bake 15 to 18 minutes or until a toothpick inserted in center of cupcake comes out clean. Cool completely and frost as desired. Refrigerate any leftover cupcakes.

Cheesy-Chocolate Cupcakes

Makes 20 to 24 cupcakes

Cupcakes

1 (18.2 oz.) pkg. chocolate cake mix

Vegetable oil, water and eggs as directed on cake mix package

1 (8 oz.) pkg. cream cheese, softened

½ C. sugar

1 egg

1 C. semi-sweet miniature chocolate chips or Heath bar pieces

Cream Cheese Frosting

(recipe on page 122), or chocolate frosting of choice, or powdered sugar.

Directions

Preheat oven to 350°. Place paper liners in muffin pans. In a large mixing bowl, combine cake mix with oil, eggs and water following the directions on the package; set batter aside and do not bake. In a separate mixing bowl, use an electric mixer to cream together cream cheese and sugar until smooth. Beat in egg until well blended. Stir in chocolate chips. Fill cupcake liners ½ full with chocolate cake batter. Spoon 1 tablespoon of cream cheese mixture over batter in each cup, then spoon a small amount of chocolate batter on top to cover, but do not fill more than ⅔ full. Bake according to package directions for cupcakes. Cool cupcakes completely.

Prepare and frost cupcakes with Cream Cheese Frosting (recipe on page 122) or another chocolate frosting (recipes on pages 115 to 119), or sprinkle cupcakes with powdered sugar. Refrigerate any leftover cupcakes.

Magical Chocolate Cupcakes

Makes 18 cupcakes

Cupcakes

1 egg

½ C. unsweetened cocoa powder

1 C. sugar

½ C. shortening

1½ C. sifted flour

½ tsp. butter flavoring

½ tsp. burnt sugar flavoring

1 tsp. vanilla extract

½ C. buttermilk

1 tsp. baking soda

Buttercream Icing

(recipe on page 113)

Directions

Preheat oven to 400°. Place paper liners in muffin pans. In a large bowl, place ingredients in order without stirring: egg, cocoa powder, sugar, shortening, flour, butter flavoring, burnt sugar flavoring, vanilla extract, buttermilk, baking soda and ½ cup hot water. After hot water is added, beat ingredients well with a large spoon. Fill each cupcake liner about ⅔ full with cake batter. Bake 18 to 22 minutes. Let cupcakes cool.

Prepare and frost cupcakes with Buttercream Icing (recipe on page 113) or another frosting of your choice.

Malt and Mocha Cupcakes

Makes 12 large cupcakes

Cupcakes

1½ C. cake flour
1½ tsp. baking powder
½ tsp. salt
1 C. milk
½ C. semi-sweet chocolate chips
1½ T. instant coffee powder
2 T. malt powder
1 tsp. vanilla extract
¼ C. butter, softened
1 C. sugar
4 eggs

Fluffy Peanut Butter Frosting

(recipe on page 119)

Directions

Preheat oven to 350°. Place paper liners in a muffin pan and lightly spray with nonstick cooking spray. In a medium bowl, combine flour, baking powder and salt; set aside. In a medium saucepan over medium heat, combine milk, chocolate chips, coffee powder and malt powder, stirring constantly, until chocolate melts and powders dissolve. Remove from heat and stir in vanilla extract. In a medium mixing bowl, cream together butter and sugar. Add eggs, one at a time, and beat until fluffy. Alternately add flour and milk mixtures to creamed mixture; mix well. (Batter will be thin.) Pour cake batter into paper liners, filling each cup about ¾ full. Tap the pan on the counter once to release air bubbles. Bake 20 to 25 minutes or until a toothpick inserted in center of cupcake comes out clean. Let cupcakes cool.

Prepare and frost cupcakes with half a recipe of Fluffy Peanut Butter Frosting (recipe on page 119) or another frosting of your choice. Refrigerate any leftover cupcakes.

Chocolate-Filled Peanut Butter Cupcakes

Makes 18 to 20 cupcakes

Cupcakes

½ C. peanut butter
¼ C. margarine, softened
1 C. light brown sugar
2 eggs
1 tsp. vanilla extract
1 tsp. burnt sugar flavoring
1½ C. flour
2 tsp. baking powder
½ tsp. salt
½ C. milk
1 C. chocolate chips

Frosting of choice

Directions

Preheat oven to 350°. Place paper liners in muffin pans. In a large bowl, blend together peanut butter and margarine until creamy. Gradually beat in brown sugar. Stir in eggs, vanilla extract and burnt sugar flavoring. In a medium bowl, combine flour, baking powder and salt; mix well. Alternately add dry ingredients and milk to creamed mixture, blending well after each addition. Spoon a heaping tablespoon of batter into each cupcake liner. Make a slight well in the batter and drop 8 to 10 chocolate chips in each one. Cover with another tablespoonful of cake batter. Bake 20 to 25 minutes. Cool completely and frost as desired.

Peanut Butter Snacking Cupcakes

Makes 24 to 30 cupcakes

Cupcakes

2 C. brown sugar
½ C. shortening
1 C. peanut butter
2 eggs
1 tsp. vanilla extract
2½ C. flour
1 tsp. baking soda
2 tsp. cream of tartar
Pinch of salt
1½ C. milk

Chocolate Frosting, optional
(recipe on page 115)

Directions

Preheat oven to 350°. Place paper liners in muffin pans. In a large mixing bowl, combine brown sugar, shortening and peanut butter; beat with an electric mixer at medium speed until light and fluffy. Beat in the eggs, one at a time. Stir in vanilla extract. In a separate bowl, combine flour, baking soda, cream of tartar and salt; mix well. Alternately add flour mixture and milk to creamed mixture, blending well after each addition. Pour cake batter into paper liners, filling each cup about ⅔ full. Bake 15 to 20 minutes or until cupcake springs back when lightly pressed. Cool cupcakes in the pan for 10 minutes before removing to a wire rack to cool completely.

If desired, prepare and frost cupcakes with Chocolate Frosting (recipe on page 115) or another frosting of your choice.

Lemonade and Strawberry Cupcakes

Makes 24 cupcakes

Cupcakes and Topping

1 (18.2 oz.) pkg. lemon cake mix

Vegetable oil, eggs and water as directed on cake mix package

1 (6 oz.) pkg. strawberry gelatin powder, divided

¼ tsp. salt

2 tsp. light corn syrup

¼ tsp. cream of tartar

¾ C. sugar

2 egg whites

Fresh strawberry or lemon slices

Directions

Preheat oven to 350°. Place paper liners in muffin pans. In a large mixing bowl, combine the cake mix oil, eggs and water as directed on the cake mix package; mix well. Fill cupcake liners about ½ full with batter. Place ⅛ teaspoon of gelatin powder in center of batter in each cup. Cover with more cake batter until each one is ¾ full. Sprinkle additional gelatin powder on top and gently swirl with a toothpick. Bake cupcakes according to package instructions. Cool cupcakes before frosting.

In the top of a double boiler, combine ⅓ cup water with remaining gelatin powder, salt, corn syrup, cream of tartar, sugar and egg whites. Place over rapidly boiling water and beat ingredients with an electric mixer at high for 7 minutes or until stiff peaks form. Remove from heat and beat for 2 minutes more. Cool mixture in refrigerator for at least 30 minutes. Spread cooled mixture on the cooled cupcakes and top with slices of fresh strawberries or lemon twists before serving.

Zucchini Chocolate Chip Cupcakes

Makes 24 cupcakes

Cupcakes

½ C. butter or margarine, softened
½ C. vegetable oil
1¾ C. sugar
2 eggs
½ C. milk
1 tsp. vanilla extract
2½ C. flour
¼ C. unsweetened cocoa powder
1 tsp. baking soda
½ tsp. salt
¾ tsp. ground cinnamon
2 C. shredded zucchini
¼ C. miniature semi-sweet
  chocolate chips
¼ C. chopped pecans

Frosting of choice

Directions

Preheat oven to 375°. Place paper liners in muffin pans. In a large bowl, cream together butter, oil and sugar. Add eggs, milk and vanilla extract; mix well. In a separate bowl, stir together flour, cocoa powder, baking soda, salt and cinnamon. Add flour mixture to creamed mixture. Fold in zucchini and chocolate chips. Pour cake batter into paper liners, filling each cup about ⅔ full. Sprinkle chopped pecans over top. Bake 20 to 25 minutes or until top springs back when lightly touched. Cool cupcakes, then frost as desired.

Spiced Gingerbread Cupcakes

Makes 12 cupcakes

Cupcakes

5 T. butter, softened
½ C. sugar
½ C. molasses
1 egg
1 egg yolk
1¼ C. flour
1 T. unsweetened cocoa powder
1¼ tsp. ground ginger
1 tsp. ground cinnamon
½ tsp. ground allspice
½ tsp. ground nutmeg
¼ tsp. salt
1 tsp. baking soda
½ C. warmed milk

Cream Cheese Frosting
(recipe on page 122)

Directions

Preheat oven to 350°. Place paper liners in muffin pans. In a medium mixing bowl, use an electric mixer at low speed to cream together butter and sugar. Add molasses, egg and egg yolk; beat well. In a separate bowl, stir together flour, cocoa powder, ginger, cinnamon, allspice, nutmeg and salt; set aside. In a cup, combine baking soda and warmed milk; stir until soda is dissolved. Add flour mixture to creamed mixture; stir just until combined. Add warmed milk mixture and stir until combined. Pour cake batter into paper liners, filling each cup about ⅔ full. Bake 16 to 20 minutes or until cupcake springs back when lightly touched. Cool cupcakes in the pan for several minutes, then remove them to a wire rack to finish cooling.

Prepare and frost cupcakes with Cream Cheese Frosting (recipe on page 122) or another frosting of your choice. Refrigerate any leftover cupcakes.

Maple Syrup Carrot Cupcakes

Makes 18 cupcakes

Cupcakes

2 C. flour
½ C. sugar
½ C. brown sugar
1 tsp. baking powder
1 tsp. baking soda
1 tsp. ground cinnamon
¼ tsp. ground cloves
½ tsp. salt
4 eggs
1 C. vegetable oil
½ C. maple syrup
3 C. shredded carrots

Cream Cheese Frosting

(recipe on page 122)
Chopped walnuts

Directions

Preheat oven to 350°. Place paper liners in muffin pans. In a large bowl, combine flour, sugar, brown sugar, baking powder, baking soda, cinnamon, cloves and salt; set aside. In another bowl, beat together eggs, oil and maple syrup. Stir syrup mixture into dry ingredients just until moistened. Fold in shredded carrots. Pour cake batter into paper liners, filling each cup about ⅔ full. Bake 20 to 25 minutes or until a toothpick inserted in center of cupcake comes out clean. Cool cupcakes for 5 minutes in the pan, then remove them to a wire rack to finish cooling.

Prepare Cream Cheese Frosting (recipe on page 122), substituting maple flavoring for vanilla extract in recipe. Frost cupcakes and sprinkle chopped walnuts on top. Refrigerate any leftover cupcakes.

Banana Buttermilk Cupcakes

Makes 18 cupcakes

Cupcakes

½ C. shortening
1½ C. sugar
2 eggs
1 tsp. vanilla extract
1 C. mashed ripe bananas
¼ C. buttermilk
2 C. flour
1 tsp. baking powder
¾ tsp. baking soda
½ tsp. salt
½ C. chopped nuts

Vanilla Buttercream Frosting
(recipe on page 113) or
Caramel Frosting
(recipe on page 115)

Directions

Preheat oven to 350°. Place paper liners in muffin pans. In a large mixing bowl, cream together shortening and sugar with an electric mixer at low speed. Add the eggs, vanilla extract, bananas and buttermilk; beat well. In a separate bowl, stir together flour, baking powder, baking soda and salt. Add dry ingredients to banana mixture and mix until well blended. Pour cake batter into paper liners, filling each cup about ⅔ full. Bake 15 to 20 minutes or until a toothpick inserted in center of cupcake comes out clean. Cool cupcakes completely.

Prepare and frost cupcakes with Vanilla Buttercream Frosting (recipe on page113), Caramel Frosting with 1 teaspoon rum flavoring added (recipe page 115) or another frosting of your choice. Refrigerate any leftover cupcakes.

Black and White Keyboard Cake
page 98

Novelty Cakes

Tips for Baking Novelty Cakes

- Serve novelty cakes on a foil – or parchment-covered cardboard tray. Cut a piece of heavy corrugated cardboard at least 2″ bigger on each side than the finished cake. Wrap foil or parchment paper snugly around cardboard, taping it to the bottom side.

- After trimming cake to desired novelty shape, use cake scraps to make Cake Balls. Recipe is on page 97.

- Cut a shape template out of heavy paper. Set template on top of the cooled cake and sprinkle powdered or colored sugar on top. Remove template so only sugar design remains.

- To pipe on icing without a pastry bag, place icing inside a sturdy plastic food baggie and cut a small piece off one corner. Squeeze icing out of the hole.

- For quick decorating, tint purchased, ready-to-use white frosting with food coloring.

- Set pieces of waxed paper just under a cake's edges before frosting cake. After decorating, slide waxed paper out; the serving plate remains clean.

Decoration Ideas

Use a variety of colorful candies and foods to add fun designs to cakes and cupcakes. Just be creative!

- **Candy-coated caramels** – rocks
- **Candy-coated chocolates** (regular and miniatures) or **round fruit-flavored chewy candies** (like Skittles) – flowers, polka-dots, knobs, buttons, eyes
- **Candy-coated gum pieces** – teeth, tiles
- **Chocolate bar segments** – bricks
- **Chocolate-covered mints** (large or small) – eyes, hats, flower centers, wheels or other round objects
- **Chopped nuts** – rocks, sand
- **Colored coconut** – grass, hair, animal fur
  How to color coconut: Place 1 cup flaked coconut into a plastic zippered bag. Add 2 to 3 drops food coloring, close bag, shake and knead bag to disperse color evenly. Spread coconut on paper towels to dry. Sprinkle colored coconut on soft frosting.
- **Colored ring-style candies** – inner tubes, candle holders
- **Colored sugar** – any design when sprinkled over a template or poured on with a tiny funnel
- **Corn candy** – flower petals, ears, nose
- **Cotton candy** – clouds
- **Crushed chocolate cookies** – dirt
- **Crushed graham crackers** – sand; **graham cracker sticks** – fences or similar items
- **Fruit leather** – leaves, snake's tongue, clothing, geometric shapes or thin strips when cut with scissors
- **Goldfish crackers** – fish
- **Gumdrop candies** – variety of objects when flattened, trimmed or cut
- **Gummy worms and other gummy candies** – worms, eels, creatures
- **Jelly beans** – rocks, balloons, buttons
- **Licorice laces/ropes** – hair, whiskers, eyebrows, outlines, string
- **Marshmallows** (miniature and regular) – snowmen, snowballs, bunnies
- **Milano cookies** – grave markers
- **Pretzel sticks** – logs, tree trunks, fences, branches
- **Red hot candies** – hearts, Xs or Os when arranged to make shapes
- **Round cookies** – wheels
- **Royal Icing** – freeform designs that will harden after drying when piped on or spread as desired
- **Sprinkles** – small eyes or other tiny details when used individually
- **Square fruit candies, unwrapped** (like Starburst) – colorful gift packages (add frosting bows)
- **Sugar or waffle ice cream cones** – trees and hats when placed upside down

Cake Balls

Makes about 2 dozen

Ingredients

2 C. crumbled cake scraps

2 T. powdered sugar

2 T. unsweetened cocoa powder
(for white cake scraps)

¼ C. chopped almonds
or miniature chocolate
chips, optional

2 to 3 T. Amaretto-flavored liquid
coffee creamer (or other flavor)

3 oz. white or chocolate-flavored
almond bark

1 tsp. vegetable oil

Chopped nuts, candy sprinkles or
more almond bark

Directions

In a large bowl, combine crumbled cake, powdered sugar and cocoa powder; mix well. Stir in chopped nuts or miniature chocolate chips, if desired. Pour in liquid coffee creamer, 1 tablespoon at a time, and mix by hand until a soft mushy dough forms. Scoop dough with a melon baller and then use your hands to roll small balls of the cake mixture. Press a toothpick into the top of each one and place balls on a baking sheet. Freeze cake balls for at least 1 hour. In a large microwave-safe measuring cup, melt almond bark for 60 seconds. Add oil, stir and cook again as needed until smooth. Keep mixture fluid over a hot water bath. Hold toothpick and dip each cake ball into almond bark, tapping so excess drips off. If desired, roll bottoms in finely chopped nuts. Place on waxed paper to harden. Remove toothpicks and decorate tops with sprinkles, candy confetti or chopped nuts, or drizzle with a contrasting color of melted almond bark. If desired, serve in small paper liners.

Black-and-White Keyboard Cake

Makes 1 (8˝) square cake or 1 (4 x 16˝) novelty cake

Cake

6 T. butter, melted
1 C. sugar
1½ tsp. vanilla extract
4 egg whites, room temperature
¾ C. low-fat buttermilk
½ tsp. salt
½ tsp. baking soda
1½ C. flour
3 T. unsweetened cocoa powder
¼ tsp. almond extract

Cake Directions

Preheat oven to 350°. Coat an 8″ square baking pan with nonstick vegetable spray; dust with flour and set aside. In a medium bowl, combine melted butter with sugar; whisk well. Add vanilla extract and egg whites; whisk again. Stir in the buttermilk, salt and baking soda. Add the flour and stir just until blended. Spread half of batter into prepared pan. To remaining batter, add cocoa powder and almond extract; stir well. Slowly pour chocolate batter over vanilla batter in pan. Bake 25 to 32 minutes or until a toothpick inserted in center of cake comes out clean. Cool cake for 10 minutes in pan before inverting onto a wire rack to cool completely. Frost as desired or cut and decorate as a Keyboard Cake.

Keyboard Cake

1 (8″) prepared square cake
2 C. prepared white frosting
Black gel icing (in a tube)
5 (.39 oz.) special dark chocolate sticks (Hershey's Sticks)

Keyboard Directions

Remove cake from baking pan and place cake upside down. Cover an 8 x 20″ piece of cardboard with foil or parchment paper. Cut cake in half and line the two sections up, end to end, on the covered board to make one long, narrow cake. Crumb coat the cake and edges with thinned white frosting as directed on page 110. Frost cake top and edges with white frosting (such as Baker's Frosting on page 112). Use the edge of a thin flexible spatula to mark lines across the cake, about 1″ apart, to make the "piano keys". Trace marked lines with black gel frosting, continuing lines down the front edge of cake. Unwrap chocolate sticks and cut each one in half with a sharp knife. Using the diagram below or a real keyboard for your pattern, place chocolate sticks where the black piano keys should be, lining up cut edges of candies with back side of cake.

Drum Cake

Makes 1 (2-layer) round cake

Cake

1 (18.2 oz.) pkg. cake mix,
  any kind

Vegetable oil, eggs and water as
  directed on cake mix package

Prepared white frosting

Food coloring (black plus
  1 or 2 colors of choice)

Lollipops, candy sticks or pixie
  sticks for "drumsticks"

Directions

Preheat oven to 350°. Grease and
flour two 8″ round baking pans;
set aside. In a large bowl, combine
cake mix, oil, eggs and water as
directed on cake mix package.
Pour batter evenly into prepared
baking pans; bake as directed. Cool
cakes in pans for 10 minutes, then
turn cakes out onto a wire rack to
cool completely. Place 1 cake on a
serving plate; frost the top. Place
second layer on frosting, lining up
edges. Add food coloring to white
frosting to make approximately
1½ cups of colored frosting and
¾ cup of black or another color
frosting; leave about ½ cup of
white frosting untinted. Frost
outside edges of cake with main
colored frosting. Let frosting set
up. Frost top of cake with white
frosting. Using a pastry bag or
plastic baggie, pipe a wide rim of
black (or second color) frosting
around top and bottom edges of
cake. If desired, create 5 black
vertical lines, evenly spaced around
cake. Write a greeting on top of
cake with black frosting. Unwrap
and set candy "drumsticks" on top
of cake.

Purse Cake

Makes 1 (8″) cake

Cake

1 (8″) prepared square cake

Prepared white frosting

Pink food coloring (or color of choice)

1 round, hard red or butterscotch candy, unwrapped

Red gel icing (or color of choice, in a tube)

Rope licorice or fruit leather in a long strip

Purse Directions

Remove cake from pan and place it on a large cutting board. On an 8″ square of paper, sketch a purse shape as shown below; cut out the paper pattern. Place pattern on top of cake and use a toothpick to trace outline of pattern on cake top. Remove pattern and use a sharp serrated knife to cut out the purse shape. Save cake scraps for another use, such as making the Cake Balls (recipe on page 97). Transfer cake shape to an oblong serving plate or foil-covered board. Crumb coat cake and edges with thinned white frosting as directed on page 110. In a medium bowl, add a few drops of pink food coloring to white frosting; mix well, adding more coloring as needed to achieve desired color. Frost top and edges of cake with pink frosting. Use gel icing to draw a flap and other design lines on purse. Place the round candy on flap as the button. Form licorice or fruit leather into a handle shape and slip handle ends under top of cake. Use gel to write a greeting on cake. If desired, add other designs, such as small round candies for polka dots or flower shapes.

Briefcase Variation

Turn this cake into a Briefcase Cake. With a serrated knife, mark and cut out a 2″ square from two top corners of the cake. The part that sticks up will be the handle. Cut out the middle section to complete the handle. Round off the bottom corners, if desired. Frost briefcase cake with brown, gray or black frosting. Add details, such as a name tag, with gel icing in a contrasting color. Add tiny silver dragees candies for additional details, such as rivets.

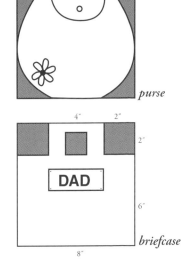

purse

briefcase

100

Sunflower Garden Cake

Makes 1 (9 x 13″) cake

Cake

1 (9 x 13″) prepared cake

2 C. prepared white frosting

Blue food coloring

Green gel icing (in a tube)

Chocolate-covered mint patties
  unwrapped (or small mints)

Yellow candy-coated chocolates*

⅓ C. flaked coconut

Green food coloring

Green fruit leather

Honey graham cracker sticks,
  ladyfingers or vanilla sugar wafers

Directions

Remove cake from baking pan and place it on a serving platter or foil-covered board. Crumb coat cake and edges with thinned white frosting as directed on page 110. Mix blue food coloring into white frosting until well blended. Spread blue frosting all over cake. With green gel icing, draw three to five stems of different lengths from bottom of pan toward the top. (Position cake vertically for three tall flowers or horizontally for five shorter flowers.) Make flower blossoms at the top of each stem by placing a chocolate mint candy directly above stem and yellow candies around it for petals. Mix flaked coconut with several drops of green food coloring in a plastic bag; knead until color is even. Let coconut air dry on paper towels several minutes. Sprinkle colored coconut on cake around base of flowers to resemble green grass; press in place lightly. Cut green fruit leather into leaf shapes. Press leaves in place along stems. To add a fence, arrange graham cracker sticks, ladyfingers or sugar wafers as fence posts and railings across bottom of cake, attaching pieces with frosting if needed.

For other types of flowers, use candies in different colors.

Stained Glass Window Cake

Makes 1 (9 x 13˝) cake

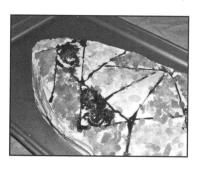

Cake

1 (9 x 13˝) prepared cake

2 C. prepared white frosting

Hard or rock candies in variety of colors

Black gel icing (in a tube)

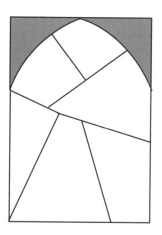

Directions

Remove cake from baking pan. Using a toothpick, draw an arched line at one end of the cake to look like the arched top of a stained glass window. When you like the shape, cut along lines with a serrated knife. Save cake scraps for another use. Crumb coat the cake and edges with thinned white frosting as directed on page 110. Then frost cake with white frosting. Place three to four red candies in a plastic freezer bag. Pound candies with a rolling pin until finely crushed. Repeat, in separate bags, with candies in other colors as desired. With a toothpick, draw lines in frosting to create the "panes" of colored "glass". (See diagram at left.) Trace the lines with black gel icing. Let gel set up for 15 minutes. Cut a hole in the corner of each plastic bag and carefully sprinkle the crushed candies on the frosting in each pane, alternating colors in a random pattern. If desired, draw a black icing cross in the center of the window. Pipe black icing around outside edges of cake "window".

Tuxedo Cake

Makes 1 (9 x 13″) cake

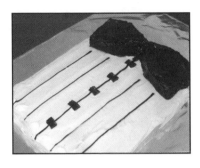

Cake

1 (9 x 13″) prepared cake

2 C. prepared white frosting, divided

Black food coloring (or prepared black frosting in a tube)

Black gel icing (in a tube)

5 black jelly beans or 1 black licorice twist, cut into ½″ pieces

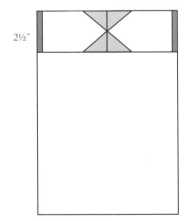

2½″

Directions

Remove cake from baking pan. Mark a cutting line across one short end of cake, 2½″ from the top. With a serrated knife, cut off the 2½″ section. Cut this section in half to make two 4½″ pieces. Cut one end of each piece into a point by trimming off a 1½″ triangle from top and bottom. (See diagram below.) Trim off ½″ from straight ends of each piece. Save cake scraps for another use. Transfer large section of cake to a platter or foil-covered board. Crumb coat the three cake sections with thinned frosting as directed on page 110. Frost top and edges of large section with 1½ cups of white frosting. With a toothpick, draw a light line lengthwise down the center of cake. Draw two more lines, evenly spaced, on either side of center line. Trace over lines with black gel icing. Set pointed cake pieces on waxed paper. Stir black food coloring into remaining ½ cup frosting (or use prepared black frosting). Frost tops and sides of each piece with black frosting. Carefully set pointed pieces on top of cake, with points meeting in the center, to resemble a bow tie on the shirt. Upper edges of bow tie sections can extend above white cake 1 inch. If needed, temporarily insert toothpicks at ends of bow tie to hold them in place. Set jellybeans or licorice pieces on shirt like buttons, evenly spaced down center line.

Butterfly Cake

Makes 1 (8″) round cake

Cake

1 (8″) prepared round cake
2 filled, frosted chocolate cake rolls
2 C. prepared white frosting
Food coloring (colors of choice)
Licorice shoestring or twists
Sugar sprinkles, optional
Black gel icing (in a tube)

Directions

Remove cake from baking pan. With a serrated knife, cut cake in half. Round off the upper and lower corners and cut a slight curve into the straight edge on each cake half to resemble butterfly wings, as desired. (See diagram below.) Save cake scraps for another use. Crumb coat both cakes with thinned frosting as directed on page 110. Cover a 15″ square piece of cardboard with foil. Unwrap the two chocolate cake rolls and place them, end to end, on the center of foil covered board for butterfly's body. Carefully place one cake half on each side of cake rolls to form wings, with rounded edges touching center of butterfly body and cut edges facing out. Tint 1¼ cups frosting in desired color for background of wings. Frost tops and edges of wings. Tint remaining frosting in one or two coordinating colors. Spread colored frostings on wings as desired. Scatter sugar sprinkles on top, if desired. Outline colored sections on wings with gel icing or create simple designs such as spirals or spots. Cut two (2″) pieces of licorice. With a toothpick, carefully poke two holes in the head end of cake roll for antennae. If using licorice twists, use scissors to trim one end of each piece into a point. Put pointed end of antenna into each hole. Use gel icing to draw two wavy black lines down butterfly's body.

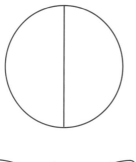

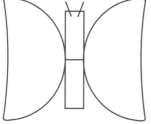

104

Stack of Books Cake

Makes 1 (9 x 13″) cake

on all books to look like the back covers. Pipe a line from top to bottom along book "bindings". Use white tube frosting to print a "title" on top book's cover and along each book's "spine".

*For colorful books, omit chocolate frosting and tint additional white frosting in three different colors to frost each book.

Cake

1 (9 x 13″) prepared cake
1 C. prepared white frosting
2 C. prepared chocolate frosting*
  (or 3 colors of choice)
1 tube ready-to-use white frosting
Food coloring as desired

Directions

Remove cake from baking pan. With a serrated knife, cut the cake in half to make two 6½ x 9″ pieces. Set one of these pieces aside. Cut the remaining cake half into two even pieces, 4½ x 6½″ each. These are the "books". Crumb coat cakes with thinned frosting as directed on page 110. Frost three edges of each book with white frosting. Frost top and remaining edge of each book with chocolate frosting. When frosting has set up, carefully transfer largest book to a platter or foil-covered board. Stack the other books on top, turning them slightly. Put remaining chocolate frosting into a decorator's bag and pipe a line of chocolate frosting around bottom of white edges

Stack of Gifts Variation

Stack of Gifts Cake. Cut cakes and crumb coat with frosting as directed above. Frost each cake in a bright color and let frosting set up. Transfer largest "gift" to a platter or foil-covered board. Stack other gifts on top, turning them slightly. Create a frosting "bow" with white tube frosting on top gift. Pipe a wide frosting ribbon around other gifts on all four sides. (Ribbon could alternately be made with fruit leather, cut and pressed into place.)

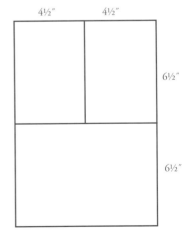

105

Diploma Cake

Makes 1 (10 x 15″) jelly roll cake

Cake

4 eggs, separated
¾ C. sugar, divided
½ tsp. vanilla extract
½ tsp. cream of tartar
⅔ C. sifted cake flour
1 tsp. baking powder
¼ tsp. salt
Powdered sugar
Jelly or Cream Cheese Filling
(recipe on page 127)
2 C. prepared white frosting
Black gel icing
Fruit leather (red or any color
of choice)

Directions

Preheat oven to 375°. Thoroughly grease and flour a 10 x 15″ jelly roll pan; set aside. In a small mixing bowl, use a hand mixer to beat the 4 egg yolks until thick and lemon-colored. Gradually beat in ¼ cup sugar. Stir in vanilla extract and set aside. In a medium mixing bowl, use an electric mixer at high speed to beat the 4 egg whites and cream of tartar until soft peaks form.

Gradually add remaining ½ cup sugar and beat until stiff peaks form. Fold yolk mixture into whites. In a small bowl, stir together flour, baking powder and salt. Fold flour mixture into egg mixture. Spread batter evenly in prepared pan. Bake 10 to 12 minutes or until cake springs back when touched. Remove pan from oven and immediately loosen sides and bottom of cake with spatula. Let cake cool in pan for 5 minutes. Sprinkle a clean towel generously with powdered sugar. Invert warm cake on prepared towel. With a sharp knife, trim off cake edges. Starting at a narrow end, roll up warm cake and towel together; leave last 2″ unrolled. Let cake cool on a wire rack. Unroll cooled cake, remove towel and spread jelly or prepared Cream Cheese Filling on cake (recipe on page 127), leaving the flat 2″ strip of cake at one end without filling. Re-roll the filling-covered portion of cake, leaving unfilled section flat to look like a partially unrolled diploma. Frost entire cake with white frosting. Use black gel icing to write a name or "Class of (year)" on unrolled portion of diploma. Draw "roll lines" on cake ends with black gel icing. Make a bow with a strip of fruit leather. Place bow on top of diploma.

Summer Fun Cakes

Makes 1 (8″) cake plus individual cakes

Cake

1 (8″) prepared square cake

Licorice ropes or rainbow licorice twists

2 cream-filled tube sponge cakes

2 C. prepared white frosting (tinted to bright colors)

Food coloring

2 wood craft sticks

Crushed graham crackers

Flip-Flop Directions

On an 8″ square sheet of paper, sketch two flip-flop shoe shapes; cut out the shapes. Place patterns on top of cake and use a toothpick to trace outline of pattern on cake top. Remove pattern and use a serrated knife to cut out the shoe shapes. Save cake scraps for another use. Reserve ¼ cup white frosting. Tint 1⅓ cups frosting in color of choice for flip-flops. Set cakes on waxed paper and frost them. Carefully transfer frosted shoes to a large foil-covered board and arrange them as desired; let frosting set up. Cut four 5″ pieces of licorice. If using licorice twists, cut each piece in half lengthwise to make a narrower strip. Bend licorice and form two "straps" on each shoe shape, pressing ends into middle and both sides to look like a flip-flop sandal.

Brush a thin layer of oil on exposed board. Sprinkle crushed graham crackers on top to look like sand.

Popsicle Directions

Tint ½ cup frosting in color of choice. Set a pair of sponge cakes, side by side, on waxed paper. Frost them together like a pair of popsicles. To smooth frosting, dip fingers in water and run them along top of frosting. On foil-covered board, spread a bit of remaining white frosting to look like a popsicle wrapper. With a large spatula, place Popsicle Cake on top of white frosting. Slide one end of a craft stick into the end of each cake to look like popsicle sticks.

Watermelon Cake

Makes 1 (9″) layer round cake

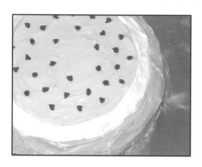

Cake

1 (9″) prepared round cake
1½ C. prepared white frosting
Food coloring (pink, green)
Dark chocolate chips

Directions

Remove cake from baking pan. Spread a thin layer of white frosting on top of cake around outer 2″ only; let frosting set up a few minutes. In a small bowl, combine ½ cup of remaining frosting with several drops of green food coloring; mix well to desired shade of green. Spread green frosting on cake sides and over top edge to make a ½″ rim of green on top of cake. Mix remaining white frosting with pink food coloring to desired shade of pink. Spread pink frosting on top of cake, leaving a 1″ rim of white frosting showing. Arrange chocolate chips, pointed side down, on pink frosting to look like watermelon seeds.

Frostings & Fillings

Tips for Making
Frostings, Fillings, Icings & Glazes

- To frost or trim layers of cake without crumbling, freeze baked layers for 1 hour. Then remove cakes from pans, trim and frost.

- Use a thin flexible spatula to spread frosting with light back and forth strokes. Avoid lifting the spatula as it can pull the crust off the cake.

- Powdered egg white is found in the baking section of most grocery or discount stores or kitchen specialty shops. It can be used to make frostings, meringues and cakes.

- Sift powdered sugar for lump-free frostings and glazes.

- Frostings and cakes covered with frostings made with cream cheese and other dairy products should be refrigerated.

- Frostings made with butter will soften or melt in warm weather; those made with shortenings are more stable in summer heat.

- To make a simple glaze, thin out a favorite frosting with a little water, milk or other liquid.

Terms to Know

Frosting vs. Icings vs. Glazes

Icing is used to describe frostings that are somewhat stiff or can be piped*
on. Frostings are generally creamy. Glazes are thinner than icings
or frostings. However, frosting is often a generic term that encompasses
all three.

Glazes and Syrups

Made from water (or juice) and powdered sugar, these mixtures are thin
and applied with a pastry brush or drizzled on with a spoon. They add
moisture to a cake.

Royal Icing

This frosting is made from meringue powder (or egg whites) and
powdered sugar; it dries hard and is often used for piped* decorations.

Fondant

It can be thick and dough-like, to be rolled out and draped over a cake,
or it can be thin enough to pour over cakes like petit fours. Both types
seal in freshness.

Fillings

These creamy mixtures can be piped* into cupcakes with a pastry bag or
spread on cakes to be layered or rolled up.

*Piped Decorations

Icing or filling is placed into a pastry bag with a decorative tip. As
the bag is squeezed, icing comes out through the tip in a line or
pattern. Disposable plastic bags or parchment paper cones can also be
used. Choose icings that will hold their shape; canned frostings are usually
too soft to work well for piped decorations.

Crumb Coating

Avoid cake crumbs in frosting by "crumb coating" the cake with a thin
layer before decorating. Thin out a small portion of the frosting with a
little water and heat it. Spread a thin layer of this glaze on the cake and
let it dry 15 minutes before spreading regular frosting.

Whipped Cream Frosting

Frosts 1 (9 x 13˝) cake or 24 cupcakes

Ingredients

1¼ tsp. unflavored gelatin powder
1¼ C. whipping cream
5 T. powdered sugar, sifted
¼ tsp. vanilla extract
Food coloring, optional

Directions

In a small saucepan, place 5 tablespoons cold water. Sprinkle gelatin over water and let stand for 1 minute to soften. Turn on heat; cook and stir mixture over low heat until gelatin is dissolved. Remove from heat; cool. In a chilled medium mixing bowl, beat cream with an electric mixer until soft peaks form. Add powdered sugar, vanilla extract and gelatin mixture; beat together until well blended. Add food coloring if desired. Refrigerate frosted cake and any leftover frosting.

Royal Icing

Makes about 2 cups

Ingredients

3¾ C. powdered sugar, sifted
5 T. meringue powder or powdered egg whites

Directions

In a large mixing bowl, combine powdered sugar, meringue powder and 6 tablespoons of water. Mix at low speed until smooth, 5 to 7 minutes. Add more water, 1 teaspoon at a time, to achieve the right consistency. It should be slightly thicker than honey. Icing must be used within 2 hours. (This icing hardens and is used to make decorations. It can be piped on for trims or shapes, like flowers.)

Baker's Frosting

Frosts 1 (9 x 13˝) cake or 24 cupcakes

Ingredients

½ C. shortening*
¼ tsp. salt
¾ tsp. clear vanilla extract
4 C. powdered sugar, sifted
Food coloring, optional

Directions

In a large mixing bowl, combine ¼ cup warm water, shortening, salt, vanilla extract and powdered sugar. Beat at high with an electric mixer for 10 minutes. Add food coloring if desired.

For pure white frosting, use white shortening rather than butter-flavored shortening.

7-Minute White Icing
(with Chocolate Drizzle)

Frosts 1 (9 x 13˝) cake or 24 cupcakes

Ingredients

2 egg whites
½ C. sugar
1 T. light corn syrup
Dash of salt
¼ tsp. cream of tartar
1 tsp. vanilla extract
1 (1 oz.) square unsweetened
   chocolate, optional
⅛ tsp. shortening, optional

Directions

In the top of a double boiler, combine ¼ cup cold water, egg whites, sugar, light corn syrup, salt and cream of tartar. Use an electric mixer to beat mixture at high speed for 1 minute. Place over boiling water (water should not touch bottom of pan); beat at high speed for 7 minutes. Remove pan from boiling water; add vanilla extract. Beat again until icing stands in stiff peaks. Spread immediately on cool cake. If desired, melt chocolate and shortening together; stir well and drizzle chocolate mixture over iced cake.

Buttercream Icing
(with shortening)

Frosts 1 (9 x 13″) pan or 2 (9″) layers

Ingredients

¾ C. shortening

¼ tsp. salt

3¾ C. powdered sugar, sifted

1 tsp. almond extract

½ tsp. vanilla extract

½ tsp. butter flavoring

Egg white powder and water
to equal 1 egg white
(follow package directions)

Directions

In a large mixing bowl, cream the shortening with an electric mixer at medium speed. Add 2 tablespoons hot water, salt, powdered sugar, almond and vanilla extracts, butter flavoring and egg white combination. Beat ingredients until well mixed and desired consistency is achieved for spreading.

Vanilla Buttercream Frosting
(with butter)

Frosts 1 (9 x 13″) cake or 2 (9″) layers

Ingredients

½ C. butter or margarine, softened

3¾ C. powdered sugar, sifted

Pinch of salt

2 tsp. vanilla extract

3 T. milk

Directions

In medium bowl, combine butter, powdered sugar and salt; beat well. Stir in vanilla extract and milk. Beat until smooth with a wire whisk. If frosting is too thick, add 1 additional tablespoon milk and beat again. This frosting may be refrigerated for several weeks. Refrigerate frosted cake and any leftover frosting.

Variations

To make **Peppermint Frosting**, use peppermint flavoring instead of vanilla extract.

To make **Almond Frosting**, use almond extract instead of vanilla extract.

113

White Chocolate Frosting

Frosts 1 (9 x 13˝) cake or 24 cupcakes

Ingredients

3 oz. white baking chocolate
¼ C. butter, softened
1 tsp. vanilla extract
3 C. powdered sugar,
  sifted, divided
2 to 4 T. milk

Directions

In a small saucepan over low heat, melt the white baking chocolate, stirring frequently; remove from heat and cool. In a large mixing bowl, beat butter and vanilla extract with electric mixer at medium speed for 30 seconds. Gradually beat in 1½ cups powdered sugar. Add 2 to 3 tablespoons milk and beat at low speed. Gradually beat in additional 1½ cups powdered sugar. Add melted and cooled white chocolate and mix until well blended. If needed, beat in additional 1 to 2 tablespoons milk until frosting reaches desired spreading consistency. Refrigerate any leftover frosting.

Quick Mousse Frosting

Frosts 1 (9 x 13˝) cake or 24 cupcakes

Ingredients

1 (16 oz.) container prepared
  creamy frosting, any flavor
1 (8 oz.) container whipped
  topping

Directions

Spoon the prepared frosting into a medium bowl and stir well. Gently fold the whipped topping into the frosting until well blended. After frosting cake, refrigerate until serving.

Caramel Frosting

Frosts 1 (9 x 13″) cake or 24 cupcakes

Ingredients

½ C. butter or margarine
1 C. brown sugar
¼ C. milk
2 C. powdered sugar, sifted

Directions

In a large saucepan over medium heat, melt butter. Stir in brown sugar and heat mixture to boiling, stirring constantly. Reduce heat to low and boil 2 minutes longer, continuing to stir. Add milk and return to a boil. Remove from heat and cool mixture. Slowly stir in powdered sugar. Then place saucepan of frosting in a large pan of very cold water and beat frosting until smooth. If frosting is too stiff, add additional milk, 1 teaspoon at a time, until frosting reaches desired consistency. Refrigerate any leftovers.

Chocolate Frosting

Frosts 1 (9 x 13″) cake or 24 cupcakes

Ingredients

¼ C. butter or margarine, melted
½ C. unsweetened cocoa powder
¼ tsp. salt
¼ C. milk
1½ tsp. vanilla extract
3½ C. powdered sugar, sifted

Directions

In a large bowl, combine melted butter, cocoa powder, salt, milk, vanilla extract and powdered sugar. Beat until smooth and spread on cake. Refrigerate any leftovers.

Sour Cream Chocolate Frosting

Frosts 1 (3-layer) cake

Ingredients

2 C. semi-sweet chocolate chips
½ C. butter
1 C. sour cream
1 tsp. vanilla extract
4½ to 5 C. powdered sugar, sifted

Directions

In a medium saucepan over low heat, melt chocolate chips and butter. Remove from heat and cool mixture 5 minutes. Place mixture into large bowl and add sour cream and vanilla extract; mix well. Add powdered sugar; beat until light, fluffy and of desired spreading consistency. Refrigerate frosted cake and any leftover frosting.

Cooked Chocolate Frosting with Nuts

Frosts 1 (10 x 15″) sheet cake

Ingredients

½ C. butter or margarine
3½ T. unsweetened cocoa powder
⅓ C. milk
3¾ C. powdered sugar, sifted
1 tsp. vanilla extract
½ tsp. burnt sugar flavoring
1 C. chopped nuts

Directions

In a large saucepan over medium heat, combine butter, cocoa powder and milk. Bring mixture to a boil. Remove from heat. Add powdered sugar, vanilla extract and burnt sugar flavoring; beat until smooth with a wire whisk. Stir in chopped nuts and spread frosting immediately on cake. Refrigerate frosted cake and any leftover frosting.

Quick Cooked Chocolate Icing

Frosts 1 (9 x 13″) cake or 24 cupcakes

Ingredients

1 C. sugar

1 egg, beaten

1 (1 oz.) square unsweetened chocolate, chopped

3 T. half-and-half

1 tsp. vanilla extract, burnt sugar flavoring or mint flavoring

Directions

In a small saucepan over medium heat, combine sugar, egg, chocolate and half-and-half. Bring mixture to a boil and boil for 3 minutes, stirring constantly. Remove from heat and cool to lukewarm. Add flavoring and beat mixture until desired consistency is achieved. Refrigerate frosted cake and any leftover frosting. Use promptly; do not freeze.

Chocolate Chip Icing

Frosts 1 (9 x 13″) cake or 24 cupcakes

Ingredients

½ C. sugar

½ C. brown sugar

¼ C. butter

¼ C. milk or half-and-half

½ C. semi-sweet chocolate chips

Directions

In a small saucepan over medium heat, combine sugar, brown sugar, butter and milk. Bring mixture to a rolling boil and cook for 1 minute, stirring constantly. Remove from heat and stir in chocolate chips. Beat icing with a wire whisk until chips are melted and icing is smooth. Immediately spread icing on cake. Refrigerate any leftovers.

Chocolate Crazy Cake Frosting

Frosts 1 (9 x 13″) cake or 24 cupcakes

Ingredients
2 T. unsweetened cocoa powder
¼ C. butter or margarine
¼ C. milk
1 C. sugar
2 T. light corn syrup
½ tsp. vanilla extract

Directions
In a medium saucepan over medium heat, combine cocoa powder, butter, milk, sugar and corn syrup; bring to a boil and boil for 1 minute. Remove from heat and add vanilla extract; beat until thick. Drizzle frosting over cake. Refrigerate any leftovers.

Mocha Frosting

Frosts 1 (10″) tube cake

Ingredients
2 tsp. instant coffee granules
2½ C. powdered sugar, sifted
⅓ C. unsweetened cocoa powder
Pinch of salt
½ C. butter or margarine, softened

Directions
In a small bowl, dissolve instant coffee with 3 tablespoons warm water; set aside. In another small bowl, combine powdered sugar, cocoa powder and salt; set aside. In a small mixing bowl, use an electric mixer to beat butter until creamy. Alternately add cocoa mixture and coffee mixture to creamed butter, beating until smooth and creamy.

Chocolate-Peanut Butter Frosting

Frosts 1 (2-layer) cake

Ingredients

1 (6 oz.) pkg. semi-sweet chocolate chips
½ C. butter or margarine
1¼ C. peanut butter
½ to ¾ C. powdered sugar, sifted

Directions

In a microwave-safe bowl, combine chocolate chips and butter. Cover and cook on high for 60 seconds. Stir and cook another 30 seconds or until mixture is melted. Add peanut butter and ½ cup powdered sugar. Beat until smooth. Chill mixture for 15 minutes or until desired spreading consistency is achieved. Add more powdered sugar as needed to make frosting thicker.

Fluffy Peanut Butter Frosting

Frosts 1 (9 x 13″) cake or 24 cupcakes

Ingredients

½ C. butter, softened
1 C. creamy peanut butter, at room temperature
1 tsp. vanilla extract
2 C. powdered sugar, sifted
3 T. milk, or as needed

Directions

In a medium bowl, combine butter and peanut butter. Beat with an electric mixer at medium speed until creamy. Add vanilla extract and mix well. Gradually mix in powdered sugar and when it begins to get thick, add milk, 1 tablespoon at a time, until all sugar is mixed in and frosting is thick. Beat for 3 to 5 minutes or until frosting is fluffy and of desired spreading consistency. Refrigerate frosted cake and any leftover frosting.

Creamy Orange Frosting

Frosts 1 (9 x 13˝) cake

Ingredients

1 (3.4 oz.) pkg. instant vanilla
  pudding mix
1 (3 oz.) pkg. orange gelatin
  powder
1 C. milk
1 tsp. vanilla extract
1 (8 oz.) container whipped
  topping

Directions

In a medium bowl, combine dry
vanilla pudding mix with orange
gelatin powder. Add milk and
vanilla extract; stir well. Stir in
whipped topping until well mixed.
Refrigerate frosted cake and any
leftover frosting. This frosting goes
well with orange-flavored cakes.

Cola Icing

Frosts 1 (9 x 13˝) cake

Ingredients

3¾ C. powdered sugar, sifted
½ C. butter
3 T. unsweetened cocoa powder
6 T. cola

Directions

Place powdered sugar in a medium
bowl. In a small saucepan over
medium heat, combine butter,
cocoa powder and cola. Bring
mixture to a boil. Pour hot mixture
over powdered sugar and beat well
with a wire whisk until smooth and
well combined. Spread on warm
cake and let cool before eating.

German Chocolate Frosting

Frosts 1 (2 or 3-layer) cake

Ingredients

1 C. evaporated milk
1 T. cornstarch
3 egg yolks, beaten with
   1 tsp. water
½ C. sugar
½ C. brown sugar
½ C. butter or margarine
1 tsp. vanilla extract
1 C. flaked coconut
1 C. chopped pecans
Whole pecans, optional

Directions

In a large saucepan over low heat, combine evaporated milk, cornstarch, egg yolks, sugar, brown sugar and butter. Cook until mixture thickens, stirring constantly. Remove from heat; stir in vanilla extract. Fold in coconut and pecans. Spread on cake while still warm. Garnish with whole pecans as desired. Refrigerate any leftovers.

Broiled Coconut Topping

Frosts 1 (8˝) square cake

Ingredients

1½ C. flaked coconut
½ C. brown sugar
5 T. whipping cream
1½ tsp. vanilla extract

Directions

In a small bowl, combine coconut, brown sugar, whipping cream and vanilla extract. Stir well and spread over warm cake. Place frosted cake under a broiler, 3 to 5˝ below heat. Broil for 3 to 5 minutes or until golden brown. Refrigerate any leftovers.

Brown Butter Icing

Frosts 1 (9 x 13″) cake

Ingredients

6 T. butter
3 C. powdered sugar, sifted
½ tsp. butter flavoring
1 tsp. vanilla extract

Directions

In a medium saucepan over low heat, melt butter until dark brown but not burned, stirring constantly. Add powdered sugar, butter flavoring, vanilla extract and about ¼ cup hot water or amount needed to achieve desired spreading consistency. Beat mixture until smooth. This icing tastes especially good on banana cake.

Cream Cheese Frosting

Frosts 1 sheet cake

Ingredients

1 (3 oz.) pkg. cream cheese, softened
½ C. butter or margarine, softened
2 C. powdered sugar, sifted
2 tsp. vanilla extract

Directions

In a medium mixing bowl, use an electric mixer to beat cream cheese and butter until creamy. Beat in powdered sugar and vanilla extract until smooth and of spreading consistency. Refrigerate frosted cake and any leftover frosting.

Rum Glaze

Glazes 1 Bundt cake

Ingredients
¼ C. butter
½ C. sugar
¼ C. spiced rum or dark rum

Directions
In a small saucepan over medium heat, place 2 tablespoons water. Add butter and sugar; bring mixture to a boil. Boil for 2 to 3 minutes; cool. Add spiced rum and mix well. For use with a poke cake, poke holes in Bundt cake with a fork. Pour glaze over warm cake while still in pan. Allow glaze to soak into cake before turning cake out onto a serving plate.

Almond Glaze

Glazes 1 Bundt cake

Ingredients
1 C. powdered sugar, sifted
1 tsp. almond extract

Directions
In a small bowl, combine powdered sugar and almond extract. Add hot water, a little at a time, to make a thin glaze of desired consistency. Drizzle it over cake.

Variations
To make *Vanilla Glaze*, substitute vanilla extract for the almond extract. Other flavorings may also be substituted.

Lemon Glaze

Glazes 1 Bundt cake

Ingredients
2 C. powdered sugar, sifted
3 T. lemon juice
Vegetable oil

Directions
In a medium bowl, combine powdered sugar, lemon juice and about 3 drops of oil; mix until smooth. Pour immediately over warm cake.

Variations
To make *Orange Glaze*, substitute orange juice for lemon juice. Other juices may also be substituted, such as pineapple juice.

Chocolate Glaze

Glazes 1 Bundt cake

Ingredients
1 C. powdered sugar, sifted
2 to 3 T. unsweetened cocoa
   powder
½ tsp. vanilla extract

Directions
In a small bowl, combine powdered sugar, cocoa powder, vanilla extract and 2 to 3 tablespoons water; stir until smooth. Drizzle immediately over warm cake.

Variations
In place of water, use orange juice or cold brewed coffee.

No-Cook Creamy Cupcake Filling

Fills 20 to 24 cupcakes

Ingredients

½ C. sugar
⅓ C. milk
⅔ C. white shortening
¼ tsp. salt
1 tsp. vanilla extract
2½ to 3 C. powdered sugar, sifted

Directions

In a medium mixing bowl, combine sugar, milk, shortening, salt, 1 tablespoon water and vanilla extract. With an electric mixer, beat at low speed until blended. Then beat at high speed for 7 minutes. Reduce speed and slowly add powdered sugar; beat 3 to 5 additional minutes or to desired consistency. Place filling inside a pastry bag to fill cupcakes or spread between layers of a layer cake. Refrigerate filled cupcakes and any leftover filling. Use this filling in chocolate cupcakes for Hostess-style cream-filled cupcakes. This filling freezes well.

Pipe fillings into baked cupcakes using a pastry bag or decorating tube and a long pastry tip. Insert tip into top or side of a cupcake and squeeze bag slowly. Cupcake will plump up slightly when filled, but do not overfill. Frost or decorate cupcakes after filling. Fillings can also be spread between cake layers or on cakes that are rolled up, jelly roll style.

Cooked Creamy Cupcake Filling

Fills 20 to 24 cupcakes

Ingredients

5 T. flour
1¼ C. milk
½ C. butter, softened
½ C. shortening
1 C. sugar
1 tsp. vanilla extract

Directions

In a medium saucepan over medium heat, combine flour and milk. Cook, stirring constantly, until a paste forms; remove from heat and cool. In a medium mixing bowl, cream together butter, shortening, sugar and vanilla extract; beat at medium speed for 5 minutes or until fluffy. Add flour mixture and beat well. Place filling inside a pastry bag to fill cupcakes or spread on a cooled chocolate cake baked in a jelly roll pan and roll up. Refrigerate cake at least 1 hour before slicing. Refrigerate any leftovers.

Crazy Cake Vanilla Filling

Covers 1 (9 x 13″) cake

Ingredients

2½ T. flour
½ C. milk
½ C. butter or margarine, softened
½ C. sugar
½ tsp. vanilla extract

Directions

In small saucepan over medium heat, mix flour and milk. Cook mixture to a thick paste, stirring constantly. Remove from heat and cool to lukewarm. In a small bowl, cream together butter and sugar. Add lukewarm milk mixture and beat until fluffy. Fold in vanilla extract. Spread on top of cooled cake, then frost as desired. Refrigerate filled cake and any leftover filling.

Cream Cheese Filling

Fills 1 cake roll

Ingredients

1 (8 oz.) pkg. cream cheese, softened

¼ C. butter or margarine, softened

¾ C. powdered sugar, sifted

½ tsp. vanilla extract

Directions

In a medium bowl, beat together cream cheese and butter until light and fluffy. Slowly stir in powdered sugar and vanilla extract; mix until smooth. Refrigerate filled cake and any leftover filling.

Citrus Filling

Fills 1 (2-layer) cake or torte

Ingredients

¾ C. sugar

2 T. flour

2 T. grated orange peel

½ C. orange juice

Juice of ½ lemon

1 egg, beaten

1 C. sweetened whipped topping or whipped cream

Directions

In a medium saucepan over low heat, combine sugar, flour, orange peel, orange juice, lemon juice and beaten egg. Mix well and cook until mixture thickens. Remove from heat and cool completely before folding in whipped cream topping. Spread between cooled cake layers. Refrigerate filled cake and any leftover filling.

Lemon Filling

Fills 1 (2-layer) cake or torte

Ingredients
⅔ C. sugar
1 egg, beaten
2 tsp. lemon flavoring
3 T. butter or margarine

Directions
In a small saucepan over low heat, combine sugar, beaten egg, lemon flavoring and butter. Cook for 10 minutes, stirring constantly, until mixture thickens. Cool, then spread filling between cake layers.

Pecan Filling

Fills 1 (2-layer) cake or torte

Ingredients
1 (8 oz.) pkg. cream cheese, softened
¼ C. butter or margarine, softened
2 T. milk
½ tsp. vanilla extract
1 C. powdered sugar, sifted
½ C. chopped pecans, toasted*

Directions
In a medium mixing bowl, use an electric mixer to beat together cream cheese, butter, milk and vanilla extract until creamy and smooth. Beat in powdered sugar. Stir in pecans. Spread between layers of pumpkin cake, torte or other spice cakes. Refrigerate filled cake and any leftover filling.

* To toast, place pecans in a single layer on a baking sheet. Bake at 350° for approximately 10 minutes or until pecans are golden brown.

Great Combinations

Take a different cake every time you bake by trying some of these other flavor combinations.

- **Blueberry Brunch Coffee Cake** (page 9) served as a dessert with cinnamon ice cream
- **Quick Butterscotch Cake** (page 33) served with warm chunky applesauce
- **Quick Butterscotch Cake** (page 33) with Whipped Cream Frosting (page 111)
- **Apricot Orange Cake** (variation, page 37) with Creamy Orange Frosting (page 120) in place of Orange Glaze
- **Dreamy Orange Cake** (page 39) with Chocolate Frosting (page 115)
- **Orange Poppy Seed Cake** (page 40) with Creamy Orange Frosting (page 120)
- **Lemon Blueberry Cake** (page 42) served with cinnamon ice cream
- **Raspberry Angel Food Cake** (page 43) with Almond Glaze (page 123)
- **Dump-It-In Cake** (page 44) with Vanilla Buttercream Frosting (page 113)
- **White Cake with Citrus Filling** (page 48) with Lemon Glaze (page 124)
- **Cup o' Joe Apple Cake** (page 50) with Rum Glaze (page 123)
- **Oatmeal Applesauce Cake** (page 51) with White Chocolate Frosting (page 114)
- **Cranberry Cake** (page 54) with Baker's Frosting (page 112)
- **Banana-Walnut Cake** (page 55) with Brown Butter Icing (page 122)
- **Fresh Cherry Cake** (page 56) with White Chocolate Frosting (page 114)
- **Easy White Cake** (page 58) with Mocha Frosting (page 118)
- **Easy White Cake** (page 58) with Chocolate-Peanut Butter Frosting (page 119)
- **Traditional Yellow Layer Cake** (page 59) with Citrus Filling (page 127) and Creamy Orange Frosting (page 120)
- **Traditional Yellow Layer Cake** (page 59) with Caramel Frosting (page 115)
- **Traditional Yellow Layer Cake** (page 59) with Chocolate-Peanut Butter Frosting (page 119)
- **Old-Fashioned Chocolate Cake** (page 61) with 7-Minute White Icing and Chocolate Drizzle (page 112)
- **Old-Fashioned Chocolate Cake** (page 61) with Fluffy Peanut Butter Frosting (page 119)
- **Old-Fashioned Chocolate Cake** (page 61) with Quick Mousse Frosting, chocolate flavored (page 114)
- **Easy Yellow Snack Cake** (page 64) with half recipe of Fluffy Peanut Butter Frosting (page 119)
- **Super Sponge Cake** (page 72) with Sour Cream Chocolate Frosting (page 116)
- **Lemon Poppy Seed Cake** (page 74) with half recipe Whipped Cream Frosting (page 111)
- **Vanilla Cupcakes** (page 83) with Caramel Frosting (page 115)
- **Vanilla Cupcakes** (page 83) with Cooked Chocolate Frosting with Nuts (page 116)
- **Yummy Chocolate Cupcakes** (page 84) with White Chocolate Frosting (page 114)
- **Yummy Chocolate Cupcakes** (page 84) with Chocolate Chip Icing (page 117)
- **Zucchini Chocolate Chip Cupcakes** (page 91) with Buttercream Icing (page 113)

129

Index

Index

Index